Advanc
Mothers and Other Fictional Characters

"This magnificent debut places Nicole Graev Lipson squarely among the greatest memoirists and thinkers of our day. A work unlike any other, *Mothers and Other Fictional Characters* somehow articulates and elucidates all my vague, inchoate concerns about contemporary motherhood—or, actually, personhood—while also showing me the world I thought I knew in a completely different, more radiant light. I finished the book transformed. Narrated with warmth, empathy, honesty, humor, urgency, and ferocious intelligence, this is—for real—a masterwork, one I will return to over and over."
—**JOANNA RAKOFF**, author of *My Salinger Year*

"This unforgettable debut forges the sensuality of Miranda July, nuanced complexity of Claire Dederer, and animal energy of Vanessa Chakour into a book that saw me for the woman I am today, while summoning the sensitive but ferocious creature that I can become tomorrow. Buy it for everyone you love."
—**COURTNEY MAUM**, author of *The Year of the Horses*

"The essays in *Mothers and Other Fictional Characters* are candid, emotionally exacting, and intellectually rigorous. Nicole Graev Lipson is the real thing: a writer whose work furthers the conversation on feminism and contemporary society and reflects a steady, unflinching gaze at the truth."
—**ADRIENNE BRODEUR**, author of *Wild Game* and *Little Monsters*

"I read *Mothers and Other Fictional Characters* straight through, savoring every elegant and assured page. Nicole Graev Lipson beautifully, deftly, compassionately captures the complexity of what it means to be a woman: the ways we inhabit and abandon, invent and re-invent ourselves. And the way she allows for the co-existence of opposing sociopolitical ideas is precisely the kind of dialogue our country desperately needs. This is one of those books I want to buy for every woman I know—especially for my grown daughters, and for my mother."

—**JAMIE QUATRO**, author of *Fire Sermon* and *Two-Step Devil*

"Sensitive, searingly intelligent, and beautifully written, *Mothers and Other Fictional Characters* gives us motherhood in all its real-life and literary complexity. Nicole Graev Lipson has written an unexpectedly moving portrait of the thinker-mother, to use her own good term. I found profound relief and joyful camaraderie in these pages."

—**CLAIRE DEDERER**, author of *Monsters: A Fan's Dilemma*

"Nicole Graev Lipson beautifully mines the loaded territory of mothering, daughtering, friending, wifing, aging, and memory, through a complex and compelling lens of her wide-ranging literary influences, wrestling with how we become the people, parents, and lovers we are. 'What kind of witch will I be?' Lipson asks, as she interrogates gender stereotypes and societal conventions, what it means to be a 'good' mother, and how to navigate (and devour) a whole life still ahead of her at fortysomething. A profoundly relatable, timely, and urgent read."

—**GINA FRANGELLO**, author of *Blow Your House Down: A Story of Family, Feminism, and Treason*

"Nicole Graev Lipson's voice is an urgent searchlight, shining across the most complicated parts of existing as a multidimensional woman in a binary world. Her pulse is daringly close to the surface, a drumbeat of desire that beautifully unlocks secrets beneath the surface of family life. Lipson's searing curiosity and tenderness mixes the exacting brilliance of Rebecca Solnit and Deborah Levy with the compassion and lush prose of Maggie Smith and Kathryn Schulz. Her essays tumble thoughts like rocks until they shine, exploring the grief of parenting, the devastation of love, and the impossible stakes of wanting. This book cracked me open over and over again, and each essay restitched my heart into something new."
—**KELLY MCMASTERS**, author of *The Leaving Season*

"*Mothers and Other Fictional Characters* is a guide to 'living our way' closer to empathy, curiosity, and love. Nicole Graev Lipson's roving intellect and fierce prose make me believe in the power of here, the whole day, tomorrow, and all our precious lives ahead of us. Beautiful, big-hearted, brilliant."
—**JOANNA NOVAK**, author of *Contradiction Days: An Artist on the Verge of Motherhood* and *DOMESTIREXIA*

"A lyrical, raw, and beautifully written exploration of the complicated tangle of being a woman, mother, partner, and thinker. Lipson doesn't swoop in with answers. Instead, she walks us through her own life, fortified by the words of other female writers, helping us see that when intellect and feeling come together they can fuel something far larger than the sum of its parts."
—**PHYLLIS GRANT**, author of *Everything Is Under Control*

"Can ambiguity be rendered with precision? Can doubt be expressed with the force of belief? Nicole Graev Lipson makes these improbable feats look easy in *Mothers and Other Fictional Characters*, which probes questions that have haunted women, and the daughters they've raised, for generations. Bringing a fresh feminist voice and a canny yet open-hearted perspective to such issues as infertility, anti-sexist parenting, and the arrival of middle age, Lipson has written the book we've all been wanting, waiting, and needing to read."

—**MEGAN MARSHALL**, Pulitzer Prize–winning author of *Margaret Fuller: A New American Life* and *Elizabeth Bishop: A Miracle for Breakfast*

"Seamlessly blending personal narrative and feminist criticism, Nicole Graev Lipson invokes icons such as Emily Dickinson, Audre Lorde, and Kate Chopin as she tackles what it means to be a woman, mother, and thinker. The "thinking" here is key, and if there is a pleasure equal to watching Lipson's brilliant mind at work it is the stunning prose that serves it. *Mothers and Other Fictional Characters* is an extraordinary debut, firmly establishing Lipson as a formidable new talent."

—**JERALD WALKER**, National Book Award finalist and author of *How to Make a Slave* and *Magically Black and Other Essays*

"'For whom do we perform sacred motherhood?' Nicole Graev Lipson turns this question upside down and inside out in this frank, thoughtful, deeply felt collection. By owning her desire to embody the maternal ideal, Lipson illuminates its uninhabitable, bloodsucking center."

—**COURTNEY ZOFFNESS**, author of *Spilt Milk*

MOTHERS AND OTHER FICTIONAL CHARACTERS

MOTHERS AND OTHER FICTIONAL CHARACTERS

A Memoir in Essays

NICOLE GRAEV LIPSON

CHRONICLE PRISM

Excerpt from "the mother" from *Selected Poems*
by Gwendolyn Brooks, copyright © 2006 by Gwendolyn Brooks.
Reprinted by consent of Brooks Permissions.

Several essays originally appeared, in different form, in the following publications:
"Kate Chopin, My Mother, and Me" in *River Teeth* in 2020
"The New Pretty" in *Hippocampus* in 2020
"As They Like It" in *Virginia Quarterly Review* in 2023
"Very Nice Blastocysts" in *Fourth Genre* in 2021
"Thinkers Who Mother" in *Alaska Quarterly Review* in 2021
"A Place, or a State of Affairs" as "Solitary Mother" in the *Gettysburg Review* in 2023
"Tikkun Olam Ted" in *River Teeth* in 2021
"Hag of the Deep" as "Macho Baby" in *The Sun* in 2024
"Shake Zone" in the *Cincinnati Review* in 2023

Library of Congress Cataloging-in-Publication Data available.
ISBN 978-1-7972-2856-3

Manufactured in China.

Cover design by Paul Wagner.
Interior design by Natalie Snodgrass.

10 9 8 7 6 5 4 3 2 1

Chronicle books and gifts are available at special quantity discounts to
corporations, professional associations, literacy programs, and other organizations.
For details and discount information, please contact our premiums department
at corporatesales@chroniclebooks.com or at 1-800-759-0190.

 CHRONICLE PRISM

Chronicle Prism is an imprint of Chronicle Books LLC,
680 Second Street, San Francisco, California 94107

www.chronicleprism.com

For my mother—
and for L, J, and F, whom
I'm wildly
lucky to get to mother.

AUTHOR'S NOTE

*This is a work of nonfiction, assembled from what lives in my memory.
Some names and locations have been changed to protect the privacy
of those depicted. Otherwise, I've represented these events as accurately
as possible—not only because this is what a memoirist must do,
but because I have a near-religious belief in the power of truth-telling.*

*This said, no one's memory is perfect, and what we do recall is
colored by who we are. "Memory takes a lot of poetic license...,"
wrote Tennessee Williams, "for memory is seated predominantly
in the heart."*

I hope my heart has been a faithful compass.

Imagination and fiction make up more than three
quarters of our real life.
—**SIMONE WEIL**

My body is full of sentences and moments, my heart
resplendent with lovely turns of phrases.
—**RABIH ALAMEDDINE**

Contents

Kate Chopin,
My Mother, and Me

My mother smoked before she was a mother. In a sepia Polaroid from the early seventies, she holds a cigarette between two lacquered fingertips. She wears, impossibly, a catsuit, and her hair falls over her shoulders in glossy waves as she leans into my father, squeezing his cheeks and grinning. He is in trouble—oh, is he in trouble.

Alone in the house as a teenager, I would rummage under silk scarves and lint brushes to get to this photo at the bottom of my mother's drawer. It was the sole window into a side of her I didn't know—the side that had lounged on loveseats and taken long drags from skinny cigarettes, smoke plunging deep as her neckline.

The mother I knew taught elementary school. She wore Nina Ricci perfume and houndstooth blazers and combs in her hair. She drank orange juice and sprinkled her food with heart-healthy lecithin. She most certainly did not smoke.

Except when she did. One cigarette a day, most days a year, for the twenty-four years she was married to my father. One cigarette, slipped under her sleeve before the dog's evening walk, a secret that smoldered on her fingers and lips as she circled our block in the dark. My father didn't know. My brother didn't know. None of us would know until years later—after an even bigger secret flared to the surface, burning us all.

My freshman year in college, I read Kate Chopin's *The Awakening* for a Feminist Fictions course. There are books that seem to glide into our lives at a particular time as if by design, finishing thoughts just partially formed in our minds. I felt this way as I read *The Awakening*, rooting at every step for heroine Edna Pontellier, the fin-de-siècle wife and mother who breaks from social convention to explore the creative and sensual parts of her being. Edna rejects her staid marriage and pursues an affair. She moves out of her marital home, with its schedules and servants, and into a small cottage, drawing and dreaming of her lover. Do all good girls edging toward womanhood fall in love with Edna? Maybe so, but in my own private falling, I was thrillingly alone.

Away from home for the first time, free for the first time to consider what rules I wanted to live by, I read the whole novella in one sitting. In Edna's stirrings, I came face-to-face with my own. During the day, I attended classes, wrote outlines, and made the dean's list. At night, in basement bar rooms and rumpled dorm rooms, I pressed myself into strangers, cracking through the walls of my body and all that had ever defined me.

Twenty-five years later, I still have my Penguin Classics edition of *The Awakening and Selected Stories*. It lives on a bookshelf outside my younger daughter Nora's room, a bookshelf crammed full floor to ceiling. There are my pedagogy books from graduate school and my Shakespeare plays from teaching; there are my husband Paul's business school textbooks and Latin American guidebooks and Jonathan Franzen novels; there are copies of *What to*

Expect When You're Expecting and *How to Raise a Jewish Child*. It's an unlikely library, the kind only long-term partnership can create.

As I carried Nora to bed a few months ago, my eye fell on the Chopin book. I lingered for a moment, her breath on my neck, her legs dangling over my hips, and pulled it from the shelf. Later, with the three kids asleep and Paul at his computer, I lay on the couch and opened its yellowing pages. There were notes all over the margins, written in purple pen—the scrawled insights of a girl I'd long ago outgrown. *Must listen to own desires*, she wrote. *Strength in solitude*, she wrote. Every phrase simmered with want and defiance.

How strange it was to discover this person was still with me— that she'd been with me, hushed and patient, all along.

In October, Paul and I will celebrate our anniversary. We've been talking about getting away, just the two of us. Maybe a weekend in the Berkshires, where we'll disappear into golden woods and fall asleep by a dying fire. Or a chic downtown hotel we can't afford, where we'll dine to trance music and fall into bed in bathrobes thick as clouds. Somewhere spacious and immaculate and nothing like our home, that cluttered cage full of beautiful children circling us with their endless, beautiful needs.

Whatever we decide, I'll need to run the dates by my mother, who will come to stay with the kids, and arrange for a babysitter, who will rotate in for backup. I'll need to recruit a friend to drive our oldest, Leigh, to her basketball practice; another to pick up our middle child, Jacob, from his play rehearsal; and yet another to bring Nora to a birthday party. I'll need to email teachers to let them know who'll be doing pickup. I'll heave home bags of provisions from the grocery store, cramming the fridge as I write out the weekend schedule. When my husband and I finally close the front door behind us, it will feel like one of those cartoon moments, the bulging closet threatening to explode the second we move.

In the car, we will resolve—and fail—to talk of things other than the kids. Jacob has fallen below grade level in reading. Leigh has been getting strange headaches. Should we bother getting the dishwasher fixed again, or finally buy a new one? The car will bump along the seams of the highway as buildings give way to grass and trees and sky.

And the terrible truth is this: After we've driven down autumn roads fringed with copper leaves; after we've arrived at the mountains, the woods, or the high-rise hotel; after we've disappeared into simmering baths and piles of white sheets and bottomless glasses of wine, my husband will reach for me from across the bed, and part of me will still be too close to home.

The dinner dishes washed, the next day's lunch boxes filled, I curl up on the couch with the yellowing book. I've finished *The Awakening* and moved on to the short stories, which I've discovered fit perfectly into my days' small crevices of calm. It's my first time reading them. The only notes in these margins are the ones I'm making now, digging at the pages with my pen to unearth answers. When I get to the story "The Storm," my notes come out in a frenzy, tumbling down the sides of the pages.

Set in Louisiana's bayou region, the story begins with four-year-old Bibi and his father, Bobinot, together at a local store when the weather turns. Bobinot points out the "somber clouds that were rolling with sinister intention from the west, accompanied by a sullen, threatening roar." The boy "laid his little hand on his father's knee and was not afraid."

Bibi wonders about his mother, alone at home, and whether the storm will frighten her. But Calixta, when the story flashes to her, is so busy at her sewing machine that she doesn't even notice the weather shift. "Sewing furiously" and sweating from the heat, she's completely ensconced in her domestic role. As the sky darkens, she finally realizes what's coming and runs to the porch to bring in her husband's clothes. Within moments, a man rides up to the house. His name is Alcee, and we learn that he's not a stranger. "She had not seen him very often since her marriage, and never alone," we're told, just as raindrops begin to fall.

We don't learn until later that Alcee and Calixta, before she was married, shared an evening of flirtation and kisses, but we sense the charge between them. Alcee asks to wait on Calixta's porch until the storm passes, but when the rain starts beating harder, he enters the house, "closing the door after him." The seal has been broken—both literally and figuratively—on Calixta's domestic space, and it's impossible not to know what will happen next.

Something quickens in my blood when I reach this part of the story, the moment of no turning back. Is it hope? Dread? After two, three, four readings, I still don't know.

The rain grows stronger, and so does the erotic charge between wife and visitor. Suddenly, they're in each other's arms, yielding to their urges with unapologetic fervor: "Her firm, elastic flesh that was knowing for the first time its birthright, was like a creamy lily that the sun invites to contribute its breath and perfume to the undying life of the world." Is Chopin endorsing this act of marital deception? Her luxuriant imagery suggests something inviolate about sexual longing, even in the context of adultery: "When he touched her breasts, they gave themselves up in quivering ecstasy, inviting his lips. Her mouth was a fountain of delight. And when he possessed her, they seemed to swoon together at the very borderland of life's mystery."

It feels certain to me, as I lie on my couch listening to the hum of the dishwasher, that only by embracing her desires can Calixta escape the trap of convention and connect with what's true inside her.

Paul and I had been dating for ten months when we headed to Portugal for a romantic long weekend. Languorous with jet lag, we wandered the stairs of Lisbon's São Jorge castle, stopping on each wind-blown turret to take in the view: a cascade of red-tile roofs, and beyond, the flat blue of the Tagus River slipping to the horizon. He had planned this trip, as he still plans all our trips, mapping our paths in his imagination like an artist drafting a landscape. A better feeling wasn't possible, I remember thinking, than the heft of his hand in mine as we gazed together at this unfamiliar city. I leaned back, pressing into his hips, and he slid his hands over my ribs, pulling me closer. Every movement was a suggestion. Every contact, a preamble.

That night, we drank *ginjinha*, Portuguese cherry wine, out of plastic cups and wandered the narrow streets of the old quarter. The air was warm, and the doors of the cafes were propped open, the slow notes of fado pouring outside. We'd read about fado in our guidebook, how this mournful music expresses the particular shade of yearning captured by the Portuguese word *saudade*, a term with no perfect translation. It is something like the presence of an absence, the ache that replaces what's gone. It's the longing of the sailor's wife gazing out at the sea, or the sighs of an old man reflecting on boyhood adventures.

Back in our hotel room, Paul opened the drapes. "Come," he said. The note of gravity in his voice made my palms pulse. I came to his side by the window. He bent down as if he'd dropped something—and then never stood up. When I looked, I saw that he was on one knee, and that there was a small hinged box in his hand, and that he was opening it.

I was twenty-five. What did I know of marriage? What did I know of time and infinite promises? All I knew was this moment, the breeze at the window, the hum of sweet wine in my head, my hands reaching out to pull his face up to mine. Is there a word for the longing to hold on to exactly what you have?

"Yes," I said.

Right here was the thing I never wanted to lose, the thing worth gazing out at the ocean for until the pink sky darkened and the sun dipped under the horizon.

At night, I've been doing research. Kate Chopin's nineteenth-century contemporaries, I learn, never read "The Storm," a story so sexually explicit that Chopin never sought to publish it. It didn't make it into print until 1969, when it appeared in *The Complete Works of Kate Chopin*. This was at the height of the sexual revolution, the same year as Woodstock and the first moon landing—and the same year my mother and father got engaged.

There are no hints of counterculture in my parents' wedding photo, a classically posed portrait of man and wife, arm in arm. My mother wears a high-collared dress of thick lace and a pillbox hat with a long veil. My father, in black tie, stands at her side, impeccable and beaming. This photo was a fixture on our living room mantle, as solid and steady as my parents' union always appeared to be.

Three years after my parents married, my brother was born. Three years after that, I arrived. Our family was a perfect square, sturdy as a coffee table. Each morning, my father headed to his law office in suit and tie, sometimes home early enough for dinner. My mother headed to her teaching job in pastel sweater sets, always back in time to greet us when we stepped off the school bus. My brother headed to his school, and I to mine, both of us in uniforms and penny loafers.

In all the years they were together, I never heard my parents fight. They sat peaceably side by side in the den after dinner—he in a tracksuit with his yellow legal pads, she in stocking feet with a book. During car rides, we listened to cassettes of the Beatles' love songs. *Michelle, ma belle, these are words that go together well.* My dad would reach across the seat to squeeze her knee. Sometimes, he'd place his hand on top of her hand. "You have the most perfect family," my best friend, Katie, once said.

Were we perfect? I supposed we were.

I keep thinking about Bobinot and four-year-old Bibi, out there at Friedheimer's store waiting out the storm. They never do learn how Calixta has spent the hour. When the storm finally passes and they head home, Bobinot worries what Calixta will think of their drenched and disheveled state. But when she opens the door, they find her joyous and affectionate. She embraces Bibi, "kissing him effusively." Bobinot has bought her a can of shrimp, a food she loves, and she receives his small gift with happiness. "Bobinot and Bibi began to relax and enjoy themselves," Chopin writes, "and when the three seated themselves at table they laughed much."

What are we to make of Calixta's infidelity, when what follows isn't pain and destruction but harmony? The woman who welcomes home husband and son has been transformed from the wife we first saw "sewing furiously," channeling all her energy into domestic responsibility. She seems lighter, more at ease. In following her desire to its fullest fruition, she lifts up not only herself but also the two people she has most betrayed. The story's final line takes the idea that "what you don't know won't hurt you" a step further: "So the storm passed, and everyone was happy." What Bobinot and Bibi don't know has enlivened and restored the whole family.

Reading "The Storm" late at night, I'm reminded of a trip my father and I took to France a few months before I finished high school—a trip that was my mother's idea. "One last chance for the two of you to bond before you head to college," she said. Did I pause to reflect more on this unusual arrangement? I don't think so. My dad had always borne the brunt of my adolescent moodiness. I understood that this trip was to be our symbolic détente.

I'd longed to travel out of the country for as long as I could remember. And Paris! I'd known it only as photos in my French textbooks at school, photos I daydreamed about stepping into when bored in class. But the whole week we were there, I was sick. First a cold that left my nose raw and dripping as we strolled the Champs-Élysées. Then a fever unlike any I'd had before—a red-hot weight that pressed down on my body, unrelenting. I remember wandering, delirious, through the Louvre, searching with my father for the *Mona Lisa*. I remember staring, miserably, at the winged statue of Nike, certain in my aching bones that I'd ruined everything.

Back at the hotel, my father ordered soup from room service, and we sat with our bowls in front of CNN. I lay my head on the couch. "I'm sorry you feel so awful," he said, and I could hear how fully he meant this. My mother had always been the one to comfort me in sickness, but that afternoon, in the 8th arrondissement, I had my dad. He sat with me on the couch. He covered me with a blanket. He stroked my hair, and I sank into a quiet fog.

Bibi laid his little hand on his father's knee and was not afraid.

Across the ocean the sun was just rising, and my mother was waking to another day in the arms of her lover.

Paul and I have been fighting. Not cathartic eruptions of passion and fury, but the thousand unmemorable chafes of married life. Someone forgot to buy coffee. Someone let the gas tank get to "reserve." Someone left a damp towel on the bed again. In the evenings, time ticking toward the small corner of the day that is ours alone, we scramble to get everyone fed and the kitchen cleaned and the kids bathed and the bedtime books read. We huff under our breath and bark orders to each other up flights of stairs.

But on Tuesday evenings, everything is different. I bathe the kids early. I prepare their dinner and cover it with foil. And then I kiss their damp heads goodbye and slip out of the house to my poetry workshop, which awaits six train stops away like a remote island. Walking to the subway, I feel that the air on my skin can't possibly be the same air as it was just hours ago, when I held three backpacks and herded the kids from the car to our front door. It feels so gentle, so silky against my legs. The magnolias lining the sidewalk are covered in fat, pink blooms—I hadn't noticed them before! My neighbor Cheryl is sweeping her front porch, and when I pass her, I wave hello and feel that I love her.

I wrote poems devotedly until my mid-twenties, when I became a freelance writer and my oeuvre shrank to articles I could sell. Now, it's the very impracticality of poetry that has drawn me back to it: I want to remember what it's like to pursue something for no good reason. The class is at a local college, and I'm the lone midlife student in a room of twentysomethings. They talk of recent movies and late-night escapades. They are so smart and so deeply likeable, overflowing with time and ideas and a sense of the possible. I would forgive them for treating me as if I were invisible, but they do not. They smile and ask me about my weekend. One of them has cheeks that flush when he speaks, two palm prints blooming under his skin. Sometimes, when I offer an interpretation of a line or stanza, he nods, or murmurs soft agreement, and I'm surprised by this attentiveness, which is like a sudden hand on my back and feels so different from everything else in my day. I start to notice his sneakers, the curve of his calves, the stubble on the back of his neck.

I start to imagine my palm on the back of his neck.

One evening, a group of the twentysomethings heads for drinks after class. Do I want to join them, he asks? It's 10 p.m., the time when I'm usually turning off my bedside lamp. Paul will be waiting up. Nora will be shimmying into bed with us in a matter of hours.

"I wish I could," I say. And I mean it.

· · ·

It's possible I once met my mother's lover. I see a man standing by the living room fireplace with a measuring tape, sliding the metal ribbon out of its casing. He's tall and steady-eyed, and he says a friendly hello to me when I pass. I think maybe I find him a little handsome, this man doing his quiet work in our house. I have just returned from a bike ride. I say hello back and head toward my room to change, imagining his eyes on my legs.

I would never have filed away this moment as something to remember were it not for what unfolded two years later. I'd just completed my sophomore year in college and was living off campus for the summer with friends. In the daytime, we waited tables. At night, we smoked cigarettes and played backgammon, feeling wise beyond our years. One afternoon, my mother called and announced she was coming up to see me the following morning. The drive was four and a half hours, not the sort of trip one takes on a whim. "There's something I need to talk to you about," she said.

The next day, we sat in a bagel shop, and she told me everything. The affair had been going on for three years. A month ago, she'd tried to break it off. It had become unbearable—she couldn't take the hiding anymore. She needed to figure out how to tell my father. She needed space to work on setting things right.

A chalkboard menu floated above her head; the smell of coffee and onions wavered in the air. She paused from time to time, as if speaking in paragraphs.

My mother's lover hadn't received this turn of events well. His fury turned to despair, and then into an urge for revenge. He called my father at his office, wild and seething and spitting out details. Did my father remember this man whose legs once strode across his living room rug, this man speaking the words that made his life story buckle into nothingness?

You might imagine I was overcome with rage. You might imagine a scene, or tears, or painful remonstrations. But my mother had caught me in the perfect place at the perfect time, primed by my Women's Studies classes and Judith Butler and Alanis Morrissette. She'd been unhappy in the marriage for a long time, she said. My father never fully *recognized* her, she said. She never meant to hurt any of us, she said. Now that my father had filed for divorce, it was possible all of this would become public, and she wanted to make sure I learned it straight from her. She was so sorry I had to hear all of this, she said.

She did not say she regretted what she had done.

I listened quietly, choosing to hear her words not as a daughter, but a confidante. I pushed away the ache I felt for my father, my homesickness for the past she'd just whisked away. "I understand," I said, which was in many ways true—and in all ways, the truth I needed to believe. We finished our bagels in a pantomime of normalcy. What can follow such a revelation? When we walked outside, I instinctually reached into my bag for a cigarette. I had never smoked in front of my mother before, but before was now just air. Her eyes clouded with disapproval, but only briefly. "I'm tempted to have one of those with you," she said.

For my fiction seminar the following term, I wrote a story about a wife who leaves her suburban family for a clan of nomads in a shimmering rose-gold desert. She runs, bare-shouldered and heroic, across the sand, wild with freedom from her conventional, suffocating marriage and a life she'd never quite chosen. At night, I pressed and pressed myself into strangers, curling into their bodies like it was my birthright.

• • •

One day after school, I bring my kids to the library. While they're off in the children's section, I sit down at a computer and search for Chopin criticism. A title catches my eye: "The Kaleidoscope of Truth: A New Look at Chopin's 'The Storm,'" by scholar, poet, and fiction writer Allen Stein. "The Storm," Stein asserts, has "prompted controversy among commentators, eliciting readings more intensely at odds with each other than any piece of fiction she wrote apart from *The Awakening*." I devour the rest of this analysis as if it were a scene of epic battle.

Some critics, says Stein, have seen "The Storm" as an "affirmation of what it means to be human." Convention has forced Calixta to repress her natural desires, and in yielding to these, she nourishes both herself and those she loves. I felt this in my own reading! Paralleling the storm's course, Calixta and Alcee's encounter seems as natural and unstoppable as wind or rain, emerging from somewhere beyond thought, reason, and the imposed morals of their culture. When the storm—and their sexual union—has passed, we are reassured that what occurred was generative and good: "The rain was over; and the sun was turning the glistening green world into a palace of gems." Alcee smiles at Calixta "with a beaming face" (his sunshine to her green fecundity), and she "lifted her pretty chin in the air and laughed aloud."

But other critics, Stein explains, read irony into these lines. Beneath the lushness and laughter, they detect a foreboding I'd registered only peripherally while swept up with the lovers in their ardor. When Chopin writes that Calixta and Alcee "did not heed the crashing torrents," that word "heed" waves like a red flag, reminding us that impulsive action can have damaging consequences. These warnings continue. Moments before the pair's first touch, lightning strikes a tree outside the house, and the crash seems "to invade the very boards they stood upon." Calixta, fearful, cries out, "The house'll go next! If I only knew w'ere Bibi was!" The storm that awakens desire also threatens to infiltrate and destroy—and in the mention of house and child, we feel the potential impact of this adultery on home and family.

I look up to see my children through the glass wall of the children's area: Leigh reads to her brother on a beanbag chair, while Nora snuggles up with a stuffed horse.

Bobinot and Bibi's homecoming near the end of "The Storm" is a joyous one—true. But the story doesn't end here. In the following paragraph, we learn that Alcee, too, is a father. We see him write a letter to his wife, who is away with their children in Biloxi, telling her that he misses them but is "willing to bear the separation a while longer" so they can prolong their vacation. Deception gives way to more deception. The circle of impact widens. The affair, we now know, will continue—and along with it, its potential to destroy.

On the last day of my poetry workshop, the twentysomething with the palm-print cheeks approaches me as I'm settling in. A group of them will be getting drinks at Salinas, a local wine bar, later on. "If you could join us, it'd be an honor," he says. He smiles, and his eyes are so dark and gentle, his lashes so long.

Suddenly there is blood pulsing in my ears, and I feel that I might cry.

Salinas is around the corner from my house. It's a shock, in a way, to realize how very *possible* it would be for me to go. Just a quick stop on the way home. I could text Paul to tell him not to wait up. A couple glasses of wine and I could be back by 11:00.

"That sounds wonderful," I say. "Maybe I will."

The rest of the class this decision is all I can think about.

My parents have now been divorced as long as they were married. Over the past decades, I've come to know intimately my mother's complaints against my father. I've heard them at restaurant dinner tables, during car rides, and over the phone from two states away. He was deeply absorbed in his work, which always came before her. He never visited the school where she taught, and rarely asked her about it. He always walked a few steps ahead of her, never pausing for her to catch up. Were these good justifications for having an affair? Are there ever good justifications for having an affair? Can we even speak together of affairs and justifications, as if infidelity were the result of logic and reason?

I do know that my stance toward my mother's decisions has shifted over the years. My parents' story is a book I reread again and again, each time seeing things differently. That eager undergraduate feminist became a woman who walked down an aisle in shimmering tulle, and in the romance of this new beginning, my mother's transgression suddenly seemed hopelessly cynical. And then that bride in tulle became a mother. The fierceness of my love for my children has filled me, at times, with rage, as I wonder in a new way how my mother could have betrayed us as she did.

The divorce set in motion a chain of lawsuits that went on for years, each injury giving way to a new, worse injury. My father grasped at statutes to soothe his wounds, as if justice were a poultice. My brother hasn't spoken to my mother in years. He has shouldered his anger every day of his adult life—a dark obsession. He wants so badly for me to share this anger, to mine its depths with him, and the fact that I can't do this makes him angrier. This, I learn, is how cracks in a family grow, branching off into fractures and fissures.

My mother has been a bold pioneer, rebelling against the expectations of her generation. She's been a coward, too fearful to directly voice her needs. She's been selfless, quietly bearing unhappiness to avoid divorce. And she has been monstrously selfish, stoking her desires while the flames licked at her family's heels.

My father has been an innocent victim. A guilty accomplice. A pillar of righteousness. A villain, bent on revenge.

Every time I open the book, the story changes. Its moral spins and shifts before my eyes.

The twentysomethings and I walk out of class into the dark, hushed street. One of them takes out an e-cigarette, and I make a joke about the good old days when we smoked things made of paper. I am offered a drag and I take it, savoring the burn in my throat.

We've called two Ubers, and the boy with the palm-print cheeks says he'll ride with me. When we settle into the back, our knees are inches from each other—mine under a cotton sundress, his peeking out from summer shorts. I have never been so aware of my knee. For the ten minutes of this drive, my entire being—pulse, breath, and thought—is in my knee. He works at a wine shop, I learn, and he's telling me about an Alsatian Riesling he just tried. I love Riesling, I tell him, which is sort of true. Mostly, I want to keep listening to him talk about it. His words pour out in a sweet, slow drawl, swirling around the car like liquid in a glass.

As we pass each intersection, light hits his flushed cheek, the curved bow of his lips.

We pull up in front of Salinas. There are lights strung up on the patio, glowing like tiny moons, and the tables glimmer with candles and pitchers of sangria. I pass this restaurant every day, but now it's somewhere in a different time zone, a different city—I've turned a cobblestone corner, and here it is. In this city, I've never slammed doors or snapped at children for putting their shoes on too slowly. My legs are unmapped by veins; my forehead is unwrinkled by worry. In this city, the scent of rose-musk trails my footsteps, and my being is a lovely mystery.

When he opens the car door, I suddenly remember that tomorrow is Nora's fourth birthday, and I know for certain what will happen next.

He slides out the backseat, and I tell him that I really should be getting home. He understands, he says. And then I say the only thing that comes to mind, which is "Stay in touch!" He waves sweetly and walks away across the sidewalk, disappearing behind a door that I both do not want and want more than anything to follow him through.

I reach for my phone to change my destination. As the car turns the corner, my chest feels like it has cracked in two.

In "The Kaleidoscope of Truth," Allen Stein wonders how one story can evoke such opposite responses, seeming at once to both exalt and condemn Calixta and Alcee's behavior. Obviously, Chopin can't simultaneously respond to their affair with "hearty approval" and "vehement disapproval." But Stein eventually arrives at the opinion that these contradictory perspectives can indeed coexist—that their coexistence is, in fact, the story's point. Quoting words Chopin herself once wrote, he points out that "truth rests upon a shifting basis and is apt to be kaleidoscopic." The key question "The Storm" asks, he finally concludes, is "not what moral judgment to make about an act of transgressive behavior but whether moral judgment itself of any complex act is in fact possible."

The morning of Nora's birthday party, I pick up her cake and balloons—a dozen of them in gleaming rainbow colors. Her brother and sister and I cover the table on our deck with a purple cloth and weave paper garlands around the railings.

In the sun-soaked late afternoon, the guests arrive. Everyone congregates in our little backyard, where there are baby bunnies and ducklings and chicks, brought here for the occasion by a nearby farm. The children giggle as they run their fingers through fur and fuzz. On the table, there are platters heaped with cheese and crackers, and Paul has put two wine bottles in an ice bucket. The kids sip grape juice from boxes, and the grownups drink rosé from plastic cups. Paul brings out a speaker and turns on Bebel Gilberto. Her breathy, tender voice fills the air, and I recognize in my skin how he has elevated this moment—as he has so many of our moments—into something that shimmers around the edges. Before long, it's an adult party, too. It's early summer, and the air feels like a caress.

I bring out the cake and place it in front of Nora, who wears a bright floral dress and a headband and smiles broadly. Paul and I gather on either side of her. I light a match and move it from candle to candle while the crowd sings "Happy Birthday." There are garlands draped across the table, paper cups stacked in narrow towers. I'm startled by how easy it would be to move my hand one small inch farther, setting everything that matters to me on fire.

That night, drowsy with wine and cake, Paul and I make love. I pull him into me with what feels like a bottomless hunger, and his beard against my face leaves me red and raw. Later, as he sleeps, I look at him. He is peaceful and handsome, his brow like ancient sculpture, his lips gently parted, his chest softly rising and falling.

Who knows what secret longings swirl in his mind. Who knows what deepest wish will rise up in my dreams. But for now, the kids are tucked in tight, and all is quiet. So we have made it another day, and everyone is happy.

The New Pretty

My parents' bedroom is still and dark. The curtains are drawn. The air conditioner moans its cold breath through steel grates. *Would you please just come see her now?* My father has been asking me this since this morning, and now he's exasperated. I stand, thirteen years old and sullen, just inside the doorframe, my fingers playing with the knob.

There's a mound on the bed, buried under a quilt. The mound is my mother.

"Hi," she says, and I force myself closer. The air is bitter, pharmaceutical. In the glow of her alarm clock, I can make out her face. There are purple-black circles under her eyes, and bars of tape hold a mottled patch of gauze across her nose. It looks as though she's been punched, or pushed from a moving car. But these are wounds of her own choosing—the blood-fringed blooms of a wish long delayed.

This morning, a surgeon took a scalpel to my mother's nose, paring down skin and cartilage, chiseling its tip to an upturn. She's longed for this transformation since she was a teenager, when she'd catch her reflection in profile and remember she was all wrong. She'd press her finger to her nose and turn sidewise, imagining away the hump along its bridge. Her eyes were golden brown with copper flecks; her hair fell over her shoulders in glossy sheets. But none of this could cancel out her nose, that mountain casting its ruinous shadow across everything.

Before she shared with me these feelings—and her plan to excise them surgically—I had no idea my mother could be anything but beautiful. Her beauty was the beauty of air: simple, factual, impervious to scrutiny. It was the beauty I returned to every day, melting into her side as she rubbed my back. It surrounded me and filled me, and I knew it not in parts, but as a whole.

Now, looking down at her, I scrutinize. I don't care that her nose has filled her for years with shame. I don't care that she's struggled for decades to make this choice. My mother has betrayed me, but I can't yet say how. Something important has been stolen from me, but I can't yet say what. I'm unsure of how to orient myself to this bruised woman, victim and perpetrator of her own pain, subject and object of my loss.

I fall back on the greatest power I know as an adolescent girl, which is to say nothing. I turn and walk out of the room, determined to punish her with silence.

My mother's mother, my Grandma Charlotte, was not just beautiful but *a* beauty, her beauty crystalized in noun form. In the late sixties, before I was born, she worked in the ladies handbag department at Bergdorf Goodman, a beaming model for the alligator clutches. I've always taken strange pride in this plot point on my family timeline, a flash of glamor in our workaday history. In my twenties, as an underpaid editorial assistant at a New York publishing house, I sometimes stole away on my lunch hour to head to Bergdorf's, inhaling the expensive air as I wandered among silk-draped mannequins. Looking for what? Some assurance, I think, that this beauty was part of my lineage.

When I was young and we visited my grandmother, I'd watch her get ready in the morning, a process that took over an hour. I can see her now, seated on a tufted bench, while I perch on her hamper, studying. To be in this bathroom is to witness a solemn ritual of womanly alchemy, and I know not to disturb. The room smells of cold cream, powder, waxy lipstick florals. My grandmother goes about her work with practiced gravitas, unscrewing tops, spreading creams across her cheeks, painting her lips and lashes. She adds layer over layer, pigment upon pigment; her face brightens and transforms from plainly pretty to magnificent. The final touch is her wig—lustrous, with regal streaks of black and silver—which she lifts like a crown from its Styrofoam bust. She fluffs it with a comb, then stretches it over her head. She leans into the mirror, dabbing her lips with a tissue—then steps back to examine her work. Satisfied, she taps me jauntily on the head as she walks out the door.

This, I learn, is how a woman comes to life.

I am fifteen and getting dressed to go to my friend Danielle's house, where there will be boys and Cure CDs and bodies that stop just short of touching. It's 1991, and I've perfected my look: ribbed T-shirt and jeans, motorcycle boots, red lipstick, hoop earrings.

But I see something troubling in my mirror, and it's not my nose, which has always been straight and small. There's something new in my reflection, sticking out sideways from my upper thighs, so that my jeans poke outward in fatty pyramids. I poke at the pyramids; they are solid and real. I push them back with the flats of my palms; they spring outward again. Yesterday, each plane of my body eased gently into the next. I was a streamlined column, a marble kore. This protruding new geometry fills me with a shame I can hardly bear.

I pull out a black cardigan and tie it around my waist, so that the sides fall around me like curtains. In the weeks, months, three years to come, each time I wear jeans, I'll also wear this sweater wrapped around me. It looks, I hope, like a casual last-minute grab—*I'll just tie this around me in case I get cold!* But I never get cold, and the sweater wouldn't help much anyway. The sleeves stretch with each tying, and the fibers thin with each wearing, until it's no longer a sweater, but a misshapen talisman of my own self-loathing.

At some point—from *Seventeen* magazine? from a class-mate?—I discover there's a name for these mounds: saddlebags. Now, when I look in the mirror, I think of bulging satchels, a lumbering horse. Sometimes, I imagine burning the mounds away. I picture a flame, a flare, a slow collapse into liquid. I melt into the pain, and the freedom.

In college, I retire the waist-sweater, having discovered another fix to the problem of my thighs. It starts with skipping breakfast. At 10 a.m., I eat a Nutri-Grain bar. For lunch, yogurt and an apple. Dinner, a plain bagel, salad with vinegar. "A moment on the lips, a lifetime on the hips," a high school friend once said to me when she started skipping lunches, and now this phrase is my guide.

The pyramids retreat, and then more of me retreats—belly, breasts, arms, rear—until I'm like one of those cubist sculptures formed of negative space. A quick-witted upperclassman takes notice of me and then claims me as his girlfriend, turning me with his eyes and hands into something holy. It's the artistry itself that starts to occupy me, this shaping of my body through my own knifelike willpower. Inside me, always, is a radiating hunger: It moves from my core to my chest to my head, a dull throb punctuated by sharp pangs. I find it increasingly difficult to concentrate. And yet, I welcome these sensations—savor them even—stirring inside me like a magic elixir.

For an English course, I read Franz Kafka's *The Metamorphosis*. I sit at a seminar table with a dozen classmates, where we discuss Gregor's transformation into an insect and the alienation of modern man. I'm not so interested in man's isolation, or the theme of man vs. nature, or the role of man in capitalist systems. I am interested in Gregor's diet, which becomes more and more limited as the story progresses, until he consumes hardly anything. He weakens, desiccates, and can barely walk on his own spindly insect legs. But only as his body recedes, I notice, does he gain access to the more elevated parts of himself. One day, his sister Grete begins playing her violin in the kitchen. Transfixed, Gregor drags himself from his room to move closer to the source of her music. He is deeply, profoundly moved by what he hears: "He felt he was being shown the way to that unknown nourishment he craved," writes Kafka. Following the distorted logic of my hunger, I conclude that Gregor's new attunement to beauty means that *he* is now beautiful, having transcended the burdens of the flesh. I link starvation with apotheosis, thinness with a state of grace.

When I come home for fall break, my parents eye me during meals and exchange concerned glances across the table. "You are way too thin," my mother says, and her words slip off me. I understand that my parents' worry is real, because I know they love me.

But their love now feels flimsy next to the force of the adult world I've left them for, whose rules I've absorbed as my own—whose rules have left their mark on my mother's face, making it even harder for me to hear her. I've seen the fire her beauty has given her, and I understand that there are tradeoffs a woman must make to keep its flames stoked.

The semester passes, and I feel myself whittled into radiant lightness. Beauty rises up in the curved bowls of my hips, the arches of my ribs. I am a petal floating in wind. Or a sylph, with insect wings.

I came of age staring at Kate Moss, the 1990s "waif" model whose feline cheeks and skeletal arms set the dominant beauty standard of an era. "Nothing tastes as good as skinny feels," Moss famously once said. When I first heard these words, I vowed never to forget them.

But I couldn't go on forever quoting Kate Moss—not after I discovered other sorts of thinkers, like Naomi Wolf, whose book *The Beauty Myth* shows how our culture fosters physical preoccupation as a form of social control. Or Audre Lorde, who proclaimed, "If I didn't define myself for myself, I would be crunched into other people's fantasies for me and eaten alive." Or Adrienne Rich, who argued that "Like other dominated people, we have learned to…internalize men's will and make it ours."

Once I read Adrienne Rich, I couldn't unread Adrienne Rich. And so now, as I lowered my spoon to a bowl of ice cream in the campus dining hall, there were two voices in my head: the voice of Moss, and the voice of Rich, whispering to me that "woman's body is the terrain on which patriarchy is erected." I lifted each bite to my lips in delicious protest.

But in the shower the next morning, I lathered my skin with peach-berry body wash until I was ripe and delectable. I drew my silver razor up my legs, and ran my hands over my slick, slender thighs, feeling them in my palms like an eager and very pleased man.

But also as myself—for wasn't I, too, pleased?

It's in this way that a woman can become folded over onto herself. And then folded again.

I'm midway through my forties. I'm a mother of three. I've returned, in fits and starts, to healthier dimensions. And I'm still trying to figure out how to unfold myself.

In the mornings, I slide a brush over my eyelids, transforming skin and capillary to shimmering gold. I make trompe l'oeil arches of my eyebrows and clamp a curler over my lashes till they bend toward the sky. I swipe concealer under my eyes and glaze my lips with plasticine gloss. I half-smile at the mirror, and a half-smiling woman looks back at me. Painted and polished, she feels ready to face the day.

Nora, since turning four, has been slipping into my bathroom in the mornings. She stares up at me. *Can I touch this?* she asks. *Can I try that?* When she reaches for my moisturizer, I dab a tiny glob onto her palm. She cups it in her hand, a magic pearl, and then touches it to her cheek.

One day, she ventures more boldly. She reaches into my cosmetics drawer and pulls out clacking fistfuls, lining up her specimens like gems. She drags her fingers across an eyeshadow, sprinkling the floor with shimmer-dust. *What does this do?* she asks. *How does that work?* She's so insistent, so desirous, and really, how much harm will one time do? I hand her my palest blush, and she brushes it onto her cheeks in little doll circles. I pass her my clearest lip gloss, and she dabs it on her mouth, a small wet blotch. When we're done, she has me lift her onto the counter so she can see herself.

She smiles into the mirror, and the blotch spreads. "Am I pretty now?" she says, and I feel an invisible fist has punched me in the stomach.

Beauty is only skin deep. Beauty comes from within. Beauty is as beauty does. Does it matter which of these clichés I summon as I pull my daughter close and hold her tight? The words dissipate in the perfumed air, lost among the tubes and compacts and brushes.

Most of us don't conform to the ancient Greeks' elusive "golden ratio" of beauty. Most of us spend our lives feeling not beautiful, or just shy of beautiful. This is exactly where our culture wants us, for we're most vulnerable—and profitable—when we teeter right on this edge, always searching for the thing that'll get us to the other side.

There's no limit to the ways we can burn or melt ourselves away to get at beauty. There's no limit to the acids and lasers and scalpels we can aim at our flesh, or the surgical vacuums waiting to suck us away. There are so many tools available for our carving. *Abdominal scissors, nasal scissors, facelift knife, lid knife*: a special contrivance for each of our anatomized parts.

There's no limit, on the other hand, to the materials for plumping us up—the lips, the ass, the calves. For the chin, Gore-Tex; for the cheeks, hyaluronic acid; for the breasts, two mounds of silicone, glistening on a metal tray.

Was Pygmalion our first plastic surgeon? Ovid, in his *Metamorphoses*, recounts the mythical story of the sculptor who creates a statue so exquisite in its beauty that he falls in love with it. He kisses and caresses it, marveling at its realness. He lays it on a bed of purple sheets and appeals to the gods to produce for him a living maiden as perfectly formed. The next time he presses his lips to his sculpture, she feels warm, and her ivory breasts slowly turn to flesh, "softening, sinking, yielding beneath his sensitive fingers." Venus has granted his wish.

Pygmalion has pined for his sculpture's vivification. And yet, even after his dream woman comes to life, she seems to exist only for his pleasure. (In some versions of the story, Pygmalion's sculpture is called Galatea, but Ovid leaves her nameless, granting her no identity of her own.) Who knows what this newly awakened being thinks and feels as Pygmalion runs his hands over her body, as pliant under his fingertips as beeswax "molded by human thumbs." Even in her consciousness, she is still, pretty much, a hunk of inert material.

Today's fantasy woman is also, in her way, a hybrid of the real and manufactured—Galatea in reverse. We are disturbed by photos of women who have undergone rounds of procedures to turn themselves into eerie "living Barbie dolls." And yet every day, in smaller ways, women fictionalize their bodies. We fuse ourselves with the inorganic: acrylic nails and porcelain veneers; hair extensions and lash extensions; color contacts and tanning sprays. We petrify our nerve endings with synthetic toxins, turning feeling flesh into cold, mute clay. We become, by degrees, living statues and cyborgs.

The fantasy of thinness—one that in lingering ways still holds me in its clutches—is just one of countless fantasies that drive women's metamorphoses. This is because, as sociologist Tressie McMillan Cottom points out, "Beauty isn't actually what you look like" but "the preferences that reproduce the existing social order." Under white supremacy, the preferred beauty aesthetic is a white aesthetic, a phenomenon Chimamanda Ngozi Adichie explores in her novel *Americanah*. The protagonist Ifemelu, a young Nigerian immigrant to the US, has always worn her hair in braids but, at the urging of a career counselor, has it professionally relaxed before a job interview. "Look how pretty.... Wow, girl, you've got the white girl swing!" the stylist exclaims as she surveys her work. Never mind that the straightening chemicals have burned Ifemelu's scalp, or that smelling her singed hair under the flat iron makes her feel as if part of her has died. She's declared a "wonderful fit" for the company and hired on the spot. Would her interviewer have reached the same conclusion, Ifemelu wonders, if she still had her thick, kinky hair?

Beauty ideals may vary from region to region, and culture to culture, but in their ruthlessness, they're alike. Women have ravaged their kidneys and scarred their faces with bleaching creams, grasping at the fantasy of lighter skin. Women have taped, glued, and surgically reconfigured their eyelids for the fantasy of rounded eyes. Women have died for the fantasy of a curvier backside, poisoned by illegal injections of silicone, tire sealant, and superglue. Beauty, I've come to believe, isn't a physical ideal. It's the promise of power, for which we cede what power we already have.

There are seductive counterarguments to this perspective. The other morning, I went for a run and listened to Oprah interview Lady Gaga, who shared how unbeautiful she felt as a child, and how she struggled with depression. She recounted a particular teenage trip to the drugstore makeup aisle. "I experimented with color, and I looked at myself in the mirror, and I literally made myself. I invented Lady Gaga. And it made me feel strong," she said. "Even before I was famous, when people would say, 'Oh, the makeup, there's too much makeup. It's over the top, blah, blah, blah,' I would be like, 'This is my life force. This is what helps me fly.'"

On mile three, my blood coursing with endorphins, I was right there with Lady Gaga, cheering her on, cheering on *all* women who claim their right to present themselves how they want. *By god, I thought, I will go ahead and wear my golden eyeshadow, and I will do so wholeheartedly!* What have feminists fought for, after all, if not a woman's freedom to live as she chooses?

But this feeling always subsides—because in the end it's not choice that preoccupies me, but time: the twenty morning minutes fussing with my face, the twenty nighttime minutes fussing some more. I think about the hours I've sat waiting for nail polish to dry, or pondering the calories in a Clif bar, or wandering the aisles of Sephora, certain some magic thing is on the very next shelf. I think about all the time my husband spends, comparatively, *not* focusing on his appearance—reading, or working, or planning, or executing, or dreaming.

What else, throughout history, might women have created with all our blending and composing? How many symphonies and Sistine chapels? What glimmering empires? Which mathematical theorems might we have scrawled across chalkboards, our gray hair wild and flying.

· · ·

I am thirty-two and pregnant with my first child. My stomach grows, as do my hips, my breasts, my thighs. How strange, how freeing, to feel in my stretching flesh not shame, but possibility.

Paul and I decide not to find out our baby's sex before birth. We know that for years to come, our child will be pounded by the hammer of gender—but for now we can live in blissful uncertainty. The growing being in my womb is not female or male, but mystery and infinitude, as elusive in its accretion as a swirl of stars in the sky.

But while I revel in the unknown, my cousin complains that she can't pick out a gift without knowing the baby's sex. My mother, in a peculiar line of thinking I'll never understand, suspects I actually *know* the sex of the baby but am withholding this information to torture everyone in our family. Meanwhile, I paint the nursery walls pale yellow and pile the closet shelves with cream-colored onesies. I purchase soft gray chevron bedding and a mobile of velveteen circus animals. In the evenings, I sit in our brand-new yellow rocking chair, leaning back into the gentle embrace of neutrality.

Then, one winter afternoon, our daughter Leigh announces herself. My cousin sends a bright pink box of hair bows. Someone sends a pretty silver brush and matching mirror. The world begins to shape our daughter in its image.

Is it possible to give voice to what I felt upon seeing my newborn daughter's chest rising and falling, or the soft, wet pink of her gums? Or what seizes me now as I watch my son sleep, his slack, parted lips and eyelids with their filigree of veins? Or what I feel when my youngest dances through space on her soft, squat legs, her head thrown back in wild joy?

Impossible—blood-boiling—to imagine this flesh starved or sliced or pumped up or sucked down or frozen or seared or told over and over and over again that it isn't worthy. I stalk back and forth in front of these bodies. I'm desperate to protect them, head to toe. I feel this need like a crazed animal.

On Leigh's ninth birthday, a friend of mine gives her a book called *Strong Is the New Pretty*, which is filled with photos of girls captured in moments of joyous bravery. Ava, age seven, cannonballs into a snow pile. Syd, age eight, happily maneuvers a bulldozer. That evening, my daughter and I lie under her comforter, flipping through the photos, reading their accompanying quotes. "Look at this girl holding a snake," I say. "Look at this one running across a field in a cape!" Leigh's eyes move from photo to photo, taking everything in.

Like all children, Leigh has fears, but I think she feels a fierceness coursing through her. She spars with her brother on the couch, eyes narrowed. More than once, she has bounded out of her room with leggings tied around her chest like an archer's harness. One Halloween, she was a winter warrior, with sheepskin boots and a sack of arrows on her back. Lately, she's been showing me her muscles, rolling up her sleeves and flexing her biceps.

Mostly, I'm heartened by this fieriness, and how it might sustain her through adolescence. But I wonder, too, how much progress there really is in the swapping out of prettiness for strength. It requires a lot of strain to always appear strong and fearless—to always have something to prove.

Maybe what we need are more photos of girls striving for insight. Or, for a moment, not striving at all—just *being*, at ease, against a backdrop of air.

One morning, I realize that my gray hairs have reached a turning point, spreading like weeds across my scalp. When I go for my next trim, I ask the stylist to dye them. Nothing crazy—just a nice dark brown to restore me to myself.

Back home, I hang up my jacket and head to the kitchen to start dinner. Leigh lifts her face from her book.

"What happened to your hair?" she says.

"I colored it a little. There was so much gray."

"Oh."

"Like it?" I ask, though I can already tell that she doesn't.

She thinks, and then she says, "I like it when you look like you, when you look like my mom," and I understand from the edge in her voice that this opinion isn't aesthetic but emotional.

Before I know it, I'm that thirteen-year-old girl at her mother's bedside, understanding in a new way why my heart has hardened. It's because my mother has chosen public approval over my private adoration, generic beauty over her own particularity—and in doing so, she has shown me the limits of my love. If I cannot buttress my mother, in all her beauty, what hope will there be for me? Why, I imagine my daughter wonders, should I care what anyone thinks of my appearance when there is her? When there is *us*.

I wish I could say that I decided never to color my hair again, proudly letting my silver flourish. I didn't—maybe in time. But there have been, since then, other small relinquishments. First,

I let go of the mascara. Then one day, the concealer. Later, the blush. This wasn't a resolution, exactly, but a pattern that took hold without my quite knowing it, the way our thoughts can shape our lives in silent ways. At first, I felt naked walking out into the world with my bare cheeks and baby bird eyelids, my dull circles and undefended lashes. But over time, I drew from my exposure a quiet, steady power—like the power of stating plainly what one means. Each release has brought me closer to the true wishes buried below my conditioned ones. I have written these words in time stolen back from my mirror.

A few months ago, it occurred to me that I hardly wear makeup at all anymore, except on rare dressy occasions. If anyone has noticed this, they haven't mentioned it. Sometimes I imagine my creases and shadows have their own strange attraction, hinting at the mysteries that have formed them. This, too, is a sort of beauty fantasy; but at least it's a freeing one.

The moments keep coming, and I gather them up hungrily, making up for lost time. I hope my daughters are watching. I hope they're catching on.

The late Irish philosopher John O'Donohue described beauty as "that in the presence of which…we feel more alive." And in a recent interview, cellist Yo-Yo Ma defined it as something that arouses "awe and wonder" and involves a "transfer of life." I like the way these definitions push beyond the pat "beauty is on the inside" maxims, showing how true beauty is *active*, a transaction that inspires and uplifts.

But the concept of beauty I keep thinking about lately comes from *Little Miss Sunshine*, the 2006 movie about a family determined to get their young daughter into the finals of a beauty pageant. I adored this movie when I saw it in the theater, as a still-young woman without children. Watching it again recently—this time on our worn family room couch, with my own daughters asleep upstairs—I was moved by it in a new way. Awkward, bespectacled Olive, played by Abigail Breslin, isn't pretty in the standard beauty contest way, but she's endearing, lovely in her earnestness. As her self-awareness grows, so does her self-doubt, and she looks to her grandfather—brilliantly played by Alan Arkin—for reassurance:

> **Olive:** Grandpa, am I pretty?
> **Grandpa:** Olive, you are the most beautiful girl in the whole world.
> **Olive:** You're just saying that.
> **Grandpa:** No! I'm madly in love with you, and it's not because of your brains or your personality. It's because you're beautiful, inside and out.

This scene surprises and delights with its lack of sanctimony. Arkin's character doesn't deny that what's outside matters, or righteously proclaim it's only what's "inside" that counts. Instead, he lays bare his love. For it's *love* that makes Olive beautiful to him, all of her—interior and exterior—in her wholeness.

I won't be able to shield my daughters from the forces conspiring to turn them on themselves. Or my son, for that matter, for boys have their own set of forces to contend with. But Arkin's lines seem to offer a sort of compass, pointing toward how I might fortify them. I used to hold back from commenting on my children's appearances, fearing I'd provoke vanity or send the message that looks are what matter most. With my girls especially, I've been careful, wanting them to grow up believing it's who they are that's important, not what they look like. But I'm starting to believe that we should name our daughters' beauty—that we, in fact, *must* name and honor their beauty if we're to have any hope of protecting it from perversion.

Now, as I drink my coffee on the early morning couch, I tell my children how beautiful they are—their fingers, their eyebrows, the flare of their nostrils, the soft hollows under their chins. I run my fingertips over their foreheads, their noses, the whorled seashell ridges of their ears. I linger over their bodies one by one: my youngest, with her tiny chapped lips; and my son, with his mixed-up teeth; and my oldest, with her one pinky toe growing sideways.

I tell them about the vistas inside them, with gentle pools of water and surging streams. And wide open fields dotted with wildflowers. And wind-swept mountains crusted with snow. They giggle and tell me I'm weird, but still I go on, cataloguing all their beauty that can't be seen.

I make myself a mirror, showing them everything I know.

As They Like It

ACT I

I want my students to fall deeply in love with Rosalind. She's my favorite of all Shakespeare's heroines, I tell them, pressing my hand to my heart, pretending to swoon. They watch me gamely from their desks—the boys with their 2009 Justin Bieber bowl cuts, the girls in their Uggs, all of them the sort of ambitious students who would actually choose a course on Shakespearean comedy for their senior English elective.

It's my first time teaching *As You Like It*, a play rarely included on high school syllabi, though I've never understood why. There's no Shakespeare tale more attuned to the restless yearning of the teenage heart than that of Rosalind, who disguises herself as a shepherd named Ganymede and flees her uncle's oppressive court for the lush and embracing Forest of Arden. There, she and her cousin Celia, posing as Ganymede's sister, consort with the local rustics and engage in the sorts of activities high schoolers love: flouting conventions, philosophizing, pursuing their crushes, cracking dirty jokes. Plus, it's in *As You Like It* that the famous "All the world's a stage" speech appears, and who better to contemplate this notion than teenagers, just now realizing that everyone is walking around pretending?

Over the following weeks, I'll introduce my students to the five-act structure, the themes of pastoral drama, and the main divergence between comedy and tragedy (in the former, things go awry and all is mended; in the latter, things go awry and everyone dies). But my true goal—the goal that keeps me awake at night tinkering with lesson plans, the goal that makes me feel the work I've chosen matters—is to use this play to convince these future custodians of the world they must all be feminists.

I start by passing around a handout: three Elizabethan men of letters extolling the womanly virtues. "There is nothing that beccometh a maid better than soberness, silence, shamefastness, and chastitie," we're informed by Thomas Bentley, author of a 1,500-page women's prayerbook—and it doesn't take long for my students to conclude that this line of thinking persists. I take volunteers to act out Rosalind's first scene: "Look," I say, "how she shatters this absurd standard with her wit and eloquence!"—and then watch with satisfaction as they scribble notes in their books. I share with them a fact I love, which is that Rosalind speaks more lines than any other Shakespearean heroine—"quantitative *proof*," I nearly shout, "of her refusal to be silent."

If this baby turns out to be a girl, I say, resting my palm on my middle, five months round with my first child, then I will name her Rosalind and pray that she grows to be as brilliant and brave as her namesake.

Teaching is always personal, but now I'm possessed by the personal. What does it *mean*, I ask my students, that Rosalind can only feel safe in the forest dressed as a boy? (I want no daughter of mine to feel, as I have, the cold-veined terror of walking alone in a female body down a shadowed alley.) What does it mean, I ask, that Rosalind can only voice her romantic needs to her crush, Orlando, when she's duped him into thinking she's a boy? (I want no daughter of mine to know, as I have, the cramped, mute pain of censoring herself to please a man.)

One day, I have a terrific idea for a homework assignment. Go home, I say, and write a one-page description of your day: what you did, thought, and felt. Then, turn your paper over and describe this same day, but imagining you're the opposite sex. It isn't enough for us to traffic in abstractions: I want these girls to feel the daily ways their femaleness constrains them, so that they might be moved to fight those constraints. I want these boys to feel what their female classmates feel, so that they might be moved to become allies in this fight.

There are few greater joys, when you're a teacher, than discovering the key that unlocks what you've been trying to pry open. But in the final minutes of class the next day, as one student, and then another, reads their homework aloud, time slows and the desks tilt, and I understand without knowing how to stop it that everything is going wrong. The boys, in the form of girls, giggle and sway their hips and put on lip gloss. The girls, in the form of boys, play football and hit on chicks. Instead of dissolving stereotypes, what we're doing, in this excruciating semi-circle, is reifying them.

And then things get worse.

I move through the room, collecting the homework. When I get to Lucas, he keeps his eyes down, shifts some papers around.

"Did you leave it at home, Lucas?"

"No," he says.

"Did you forget to do it?"

"No," he says.

Lucas is one of the most diligent students I've ever had, and in the best of ways, because his diligence has nothing to do with college applications or compliance but with a deep and driving desire to really *get* things. He has never, in the two years I've been his teacher, failed to turn in work.

The room has emptied, and it's just the two of us. Silence. Florescent light. Something is wrong. Something raw and beating hangs in the space between us. I do not know what this thing is or how to draw it out so I can tend to it.

"Can you help me out a little?" I try.

He looks at me. There are freckles on his nose, curtains of hair across his forehead. Behind his glasses, his eyes are two hazel pools. "It was just too hard," he says, "to write about this topic."

I am not understanding. The air is thick with my lack of understanding.

"Too hard?"

He looks up at the ceiling and takes a breath. "Too hard," he goes on, "because I think about it every day of my life. All I want is for my brain to stop fucking thinking about it."

His words pool in my ears and linger there. And because it is the first decade of the new century—because Caitlyn Jenner is not yet Caitlyn Jenner and public bathrooms are not yet the focus of op-eds, and pronouns are only on my radar when I'm planning grammar lessons; because my softness pleases me and my curves please me and the secret sinuous parts of me please me and I've had no reason to imagine what my life would be like if they didn't; and because it has never once occurred to me, inside the tunnel of my own agenda, that Rosalind might yearn for something other than equality when she slips into the clothes of a man—it takes far longer than it should for me to grasp what he is telling me.

"I see, Lucas," I say. "I see."

But the truth is, I was just then beginning to see.

I had no idea how hard it would be to see.

ACT II

When our daughter is born, we do not name her Rosalind, but she takes after my favorite heroine nonetheless. She announces her needs with muscular cries, grabs onto the world with determined fists. Like Rosalind, she delights in humor, grinning as she bites her toes on the changing table, and toppling with laughter when we pretend to drink from her bottle. And she loves, like Rosalind, to talk: in coos, in words, in paragraphs—in romping soliloquies delivered from the back of the car. She is sprightly and clever, can keep up with the quickest of clowns.

So we're a little confused, when Leigh starts kindergarten, that she seems to have such trouble making friends. She hunkers beside me on the playground bench as her classmates gallop by, grows sullen when I suggest she join a couple of girls on the swings. The scene before her beckons, joyous and wheeling, but something is keeping her watching, trapped in the wings.

When she finally makes a friend, I'm deeply relieved. Zeke loves Han Solo and the Beast Quest fantasy series like her, and when they joust with their homemade lightsabers in our kitchen, their laughs are indistinguishable. Through Zeke, Leigh becomes friends with Miles, and then with Daniel and Jinhai, Tobias and

Max, and before long, she has a true and proper crew. She looks forward to school, and her face shines, and she is happy.

I've never been a fan of the label "tomboy"—the way it suggests there's only one real way to be a girl. And yet, can we ever fully escape the language we've been handed to map our world? My daughter becomes, before my eyes, a tomboy, for this is the most familiar way I have to see her. And in truth, I take a little pride in her tomboyishness—have maybe even encouraged it, careful not to read her books like *Fancy Nancy* and *Pinkalicious*, careful not to *ooh* and *aah* over the way her skirt twirls. Unlike the beribboned Nancy in her dress-up heels, a girl who can run with the boys is slightly renegade, like the gutsy heroines from my favorite children's classics: Jo March, getting into "scrapes" and sullying her petticoats, or Scout in her overalls, rolling in tires. She's a girl who has dared to cast off the limits imposed on her.

Rosalind goes a step further than these tomboy heroines when she decides not simply to act like a boy but to impersonate one. By the end of *As You Like It*'s first act, her ruthless uncle has usurped her father's throne, sent him into hiding, and banished her from his court: Rosalind, in other words, has been completely undone by patriarchy. Despondent, she speaks in listless monosyllables as she and Celia plan their escape to Arden—until she has an invigorating idea: Wouldn't it be wonderful, she suggests, her phrases lengthening, her imagery gathering energy, "That I did suit me all points like a man? / A gallant curtle-axe upon my thigh, / A boar-spear in my hand." No matter how terrified she is on their journey, she proclaims, she'll project "a swashing and a martial outside, / As many other mannish cowards have / That do outface it with their semblances." Centuries before Judith Butler, here is Rosalind, surmising in her own whimsical way that gender is a performance.

But once she's actually in costume, traveling through the forest, something interesting happens: Her emotional landscape shifts to align with her male attire. "I could find it in my heart to disgrace my man's apparel and cry like a woman," she announces to Celia when they arrive, exhausted, in Arden. "But," she goes on, "I must comfort the weaker vessel, as doublet and hose ought to show itself courageous to petticoat." Her masculine clothing rouses something in her, and she rises above her own distress to encourage her cousin onward. This might seem like a moment of virtuoso acting on Rosalind's part—the consummate Butlerian performance. But is it really? The inner strength she summons is, after all, *her* strength. Freed from the corsets and costumery of womanhood, it isn't manhood Rosalind steps into, but her truest self.

This is the version of Rosalind that lives in me as I watch Leigh on the playground one fall afternoon in first grade. She and a throng of classmates have organized a chasing game, boys against girls—and she is on the boys' team. She rockets through leaves, shouting commands to her teammates, shins streaked with dirt, ponytail whipping in the wind. On the boys' team, my daughter scales slides like mountains and stretches her limbs to her soul's horizons. On the boys' team, she's the powerful girl she is.

This is the Rosalind I carry in my heart one year later, when Leigh comes down to breakfast in her little brother's clothes: cargo shorts and button-down shirt, shark-tooth necklace and baseball cap. Seconds later, Jacob comes trailing behind in *her* clothes: a gold headband and dotted leggings and the yellow eyelet skirt my mother bought her for special occasions. He spins and prances and howls with laughter—there isn't room in his body to contain how hilarious this is. But Leigh, in the hallway mirror, does not laugh. She narrows her eyes, turns her hat backward. In boys' clothes, she is the cool, slick girl she is.

And when my daughter starts third grade, this is the Rosalind I see her through, like a transparent overlay, as we wander through Target looking for back-to-school clothes. She walks down the bubblegum aisles of the girls' section, past sequined T-shirts and ruffled sweatshirts—circling and circling, scanning, searching—and then drifts into the rugged outback of the boys' section, where she pulls item after item from the shelves until her arms are loaded. In the boys' section, my daughter claims what hasn't been offered to her. In the boys' section, she's the dissident girl she is.

I know this plot so well, and I'm a sucker for it—the one about the girl who finds, in the trappings of boyhood, her ticket to autonomy. Rosalind is hardly the only fictional maiden who cross-dresses her way to emancipation. She isn't even the only one conceived by Shakespeare, who also gave us Imogen and Julia, Viola in her servant's livery, and Portia in her lawyer's robes. Centuries before Rosalind there was Athena, who appeared in male guise to assist Odysseus, and Ovid's Iphis, whose mother raised her as a boy to save her from infanticide. And centuries later came her many film successors, like Disney's Mulan, who poses as a soldier to save her father from conscription in the army; Terry from the '80s teen flick *Just One of the Guys*, who masquerades as a boy to get an edge in a high school internship competition; and Viola of the *Twelfth Night*–inspired comedy *She's the Man*, who impersonates her brother so she can play boarding school soccer after the girls' team has been cut.

This storyline, like the conditions that give rise to it, isn't just the stuff of fiction. Think of the female authors—the Brontë sisters and George Eliot and George Sand and Isak Dinesen and

P. L. Travers and P. D. James—who've assumed masculine pen names to get their voices heard. The Victorian surgeon Margaret Ann Bulkley lived for years as "Dr. James Barry" so she could practice medicine. Kathrine Switzer became the first woman to register and run in the Boston Marathon, using just her first and middle initials to sneak past the ban on female athletes. Rachel Balkovec broke into the male-dominated dugouts of professional baseball by using the name "Rae" on her resume, eventually becoming the first female manager in the history of the minor leagues.

When we get home from Target, Leigh spills her new clothes onto the breakfast table. And then, right there in our kitchen, she tugs and shimmies her way into them one by one: the stovepipe jeans, the pocket T-shirt, the baggy hoodie, the navy parka. As she zips and snaps herself in, her cheeks pinkening, her eyes brightening, I see a girl who is doing what she can to unleash her powers and hold tight to her fate. This is a story that makes sense to me, a story I can get behind.

And like Switzer, Mulan, Rosalind, and all the other cross-dressing heroines who've captured my imagination, my daughter, too, I assume, will one day reach the part of the story when her disguise has served its purpose. Her courage revealed, her ambitions realized, she will slough off her costume like a rumpled cocoon. And then, true to the tomboy canon, she will stand, plain and proud, in the truth of who she is—the beautiful, flesh-and-blood girl I birthed into the world.

ACT III

In 1599, the year Shakespeare wrote *As You Like It*, wearing male clothing was becoming something of a trend among urban English women. Emboldened by the increased social mobility that accompanied the earliest stirrings of capitalism, many appeared in public donning cloaks, doublets, feathered hats, and other mannish trappings—a practice that didn't go over well with England's ruling class, who understood how this threatened their patriarchal authority. Ministers, under the order of James I, invoked Deuteronomy as they warned their parishioners that "The woman shall not wear that which pertaineth unto a man...for all that do so are an abomination unto the Lord thy God." Those who violated this command risked being whipped or pilloried by London's magistrates.

In fourth grade my daughter does not abandon her costume. As she enters fifth grade, she does not abandon her costume. At what age, had she lived in early modern England, would she have been old enough to be punished for her transgression?

I'm grateful to live in a decade and country where we can clothe ourselves as we like with less chance of arrest. But as Leigh's tomboy phase stretches into early adolescence, my pride becomes more measured. I'm unsettled to notice how the "girl" things of this world she's simply done without have become, over time, the targets of her snarkiest derision. She snorts at her little sister's hair bows, says "Ewww..." when she ends up with the pink mug at breakfast. Where's the line, I begin to wonder, between a healthy rejection of female stereotypes and misogyny absorbed and turned inward? This thought nags at me, making me long to see my daughter find strength and vitality *inside* her girlhood rather than on the lam from it.

Rosalind, too, is in no rush to give up her masculine presentation, pretending to be Ganymede long after her disguise has served its purpose. She's made it to Arden unscathed, ingratiated herself with the locals, and settled happily into country living—and still she maintains the ruse. And who could blame her? Not only does her costume unleash her buried courage and powers of expression, but it enables her to do the unthinkable for a woman at the time and acquire her own property, a working farm she buys from a local shepherd.

Rosalind decides to prolong her performance even further when she discovers that the dashing Orlando, whom she recently met at court, is also in the forest, where he's come to escape his murderous brother. Though she's spoken with Orlando only once, the encounter was enough to leave her besotted. And she's thrilled to learn—as she stumbles upon the love poems he's penned in her honor and strewn from Arden's trees—that their conversation left him just as smitten. "Alas the day, what shall I do with my doublet and hose?" she exclaims to Celia when she learns Orlando is close by. Resuming their flirtation, she realizes, will mean relinquishing her disguise.

But when Orlando wanders onto the scene moments later, she makes the split-second decision to stay in character. "I will speak to him like a saucy lackey," she whispers to Celia, "and under that habit play the knave with him." As Ganymede, Rosalind can be her most audacious self with Orlando, and her agile mind is on peak display in the verbal jousting that follows. By the time the two part, she's come up with an idea that will allow her to enjoy both the freedom of her male persona *and* the romantic energy between her and Orlando. What he must do, Rosalind-as-Ganymede tells him, is submit to her no-fail remedy for lovesickness, which turns out to be a sort of rudimentary form of psychodrama therapy: She can "cure" him, she says, if he agrees to call her Rosalind and visit her daily, pretending to woo her.

As the pair carry out this plan, we see a near-total reversal of the conventional dynamics of courtship. Orlando may seem, in their role-play, to be the pursuer, but it's Rosalind who truly holds the power, prescribing for Orlando the moves he should make and the words he should utter. As Ganymede, Rosalind slowly shapes him into the lover she wishes him to be—a little less melodramatic, a little more clear-sighted. Her schooling makes him worthy, by the play's end, of the restoration of her female identity and her hand in marriage.

I remember watching a performance of *As You Like It* on the Boston Common nearly fifteen years ago, pre-motherhood, grinning in the summer dusk as the actress playing Rosalind embodied, superbly, her character's fiendish thrill at upending the gender norms of romance. But I think if I were to attend this same production now, I might be even more compelled by the brief scene that follows, in which Celia lays into Rosalind for the sexist jokes she's been making to Orlando "man-to-man." "You have simply misused our sex in your love-prate," she exclaims, berating her treasonous cousin for what she's "done to her own nest."

These are the words I would hang on now, from my blanket on the grass, for there would be—if not in the flesh, then in my thoughts—my daughter sitting beside me, with her lanky legs and enormous high tops, her rounding hips and boxy track shorts, leaving me doubting whether freedom based on a double standard is freedom at all. And there would be, underneath this, a far less abstract fear: that in trying to stop the world from turning my daughter into the girl it wants her to be, I've sent the message there's something wrong with being a girl altogether.

If you've known the corrosive burden of second-guessing the lessons you've imparted as a parent, maybe you'll understand my relief when, in the fall of fifth grade, Leigh makes friends with a group of girls she adores. Maybe you'll understand how my entire body lightens when these girls come to our house for a sleepover, where they paint squish-toys shaped like ice cream cones and stir up brimming bowls of rainbow slime. Maybe you'll understand the absolution I feel when I open my email, one day, to find a link to a floral romper Leigh hopes I will buy her.

Let me describe what I feel when my daughter appears in my doorway asking, for the first time ever, if I'll French-braid her hair. We sit down on my rug, and I run my hands through her waves, feeling them tumble, thick and silky, between my fingers. I weave one section over another, gathering in more strands, smoothing down my work. And as I do, I am flooded by a memory of sitting in front of my own mother at her dressing table, feeling her slip barrettes into place behind my temples. The air is fragrant from her shower and warm from her rollers, and I feel cared for and anointed in a way that feels distinctly feminine in the tending of one female body by another. I have returned, on this rug, to my own lived version of maidenhood, familiar and comforting as my mother's touch. I take in the pale curve of Leigh's neck, the smooth edge of her shoulder, and am seized by possessive wonder at this miracle of a girl, in whose lineaments I recognize my own.

I have no idea that, just three months later, Leigh will give away her floral romper to her little sister, though Nora is half a decade away from fitting into it. I have no idea that I will sit behind her during the salon appointment she has begged me to make for her, watching her hair drop in long, dark sheafs to the floor.

ACT IV

"All the world's a stage, / And all the men and women merely players," observes Jaques, the secondary character who utters *As You Like It*'s most renowned words. The summer of 2021, when Leigh crops her hair an inch from her head, is the summer a curtain opens, and she steps out onto the set a different character. The entire theater we inhabit, in fact, has been transformed. It seems to me that the world until this moment followed one set of logic, and now it follows a different logic, as if I've been transported in the dark of night to an upside-down realm.

The summer Leigh cuts off nearly all her hair is the summer she asks me what my favorite boys' names are. It's the summer a friend's nephew starts to go by *she*, and Cora from around the corner starts to go by *he*, and a classmate of Leigh's starts to go by *she* some days and *he* on others. It's the summer I can no longer keep Leigh's friends' names straight, for Caroline has become Cal and then Coby, and when April arrives at our house for dinner, I learn that he's Aiden. Our days become a pageant of exits and entrances, everyone coming and going in different form.

It's during this summer, before the start of sixth grade, that Leigh teaches me about Bitmojis, the cute digital avatars you can customize. She shows me how they work, scrolling through the selection categories. There are options for gender and options for age, options for skin tone and options for body type, options for pants and skirts and shoes and hats and scarves and belts and gloves and glasses and rings and watches. She helps me make my own Bitmoji, and I get a little window into the fun of it, this limitless choose-your-own adventure of personal identity. "Want to see mine?" Leigh asks, and with a touch of a finger there she is: a rakish mop-headed kid in a striped rugby jersey, sneakers planted firmly on the ground.

The summer of Leigh's haircut marks the start of a perpetual season of mistaken identity. "What can I get for you, buddy?" a Starbucks barista asks her that August. "Morning, sir," says the friendly crossing guard that fall. One Saturday the following winter, our family walks to a nearby synagogue to attend a bat mitzvah. As Leigh climbs the steps in her boots and bulky parka, the security guard gives her a thumbs-up: "You keeping everyone protected, Muscles?" he says. Nothing in her expression helps me understand how she feels about these greetings.

Do I consider, as my daughter's body reshapes itself under her winter layers into woman form, that perhaps this isn't a passing phase at all? Do I wonder, when I behold her avatar, what deeper, unspoken longings it might contain? I do—more and more every day, I do—for in 2021, discussions of gender identity are everywhere: in curricula and lectures and PTA meetings and board meetings and broadcasts and podcasts and the pages of celebrity magazines, where Demi Lovato has revealed they're nonbinary and Elliot Page has opened up about claiming his male identity.

I think often, during this cultural efflorescence, of my student Lucas—the caged pain in his eyes, the courage it must have taken him to break the silence between us—and how much easier his teen years may have been had he been born just one decade later.

I wonder where Lucas is now, and whether he's found his way to comfort and wholeness. My hopes for Lucas's happiness are surprisingly strong given how long it's been since I knew him—and far simpler than the mix of emotions that churns in me as I watch my daughter's spirit converge with the fervors of her era.

Leigh is my child, yes: It's natural that my relationship to her identity would be more complicated. But my preoccupations are more specific than this. I can't stop thinking, for instance, about a particular *Slate* article reporting that in the past two decades, trans youth clinics in North America and Europe have begun seeing more patients transitioning from female to male than vice versa—a significant change from prior years. Researchers aren't certain what's behind this shift, but one thing I think about as I read, which the piece doesn't mention, is the difference between what it means to live as man and to live as woman—a difference that, since 2016, has only become grimmer for women. "How gender identities are constituted and how specific brands of sexuality are formed," writes scholar Keith Thomas in a reissued 1994 *New York Review of Books* essay I come across about queer undercurrents in Renaissance texts, "are issues that are inseparably connected with the structure of power and the working of society in all its dimensions." Changing gender is never a power-neutral conversion—a truth my friend Mira hinted at, less eloquently, after the reversal of *Roe v. Wade*, when she said, "I never doubt that trans women are women, because why the hell would someone *choose* to become a woman in our fucked-up patriarchy?"

I laughed awkwardly at this comment, unsure if it was the sort of thing we're allowed to say as well-meaning liberals in a well-meaning liberal Boston suburb. I'm no longer certain what I can and cannot say, but more often than ever lately, I suspect that what I'm thinking falls in the latter category. I should not wonder aloud—as Paul and I have in private—whether the drastic uptick in transgender youth might in some part reflect a rising preference for gender-bending as the particular teen reinvention mode of the moment, the way I briefly became a Goth in 1992, or speculate that all these name changes must be hard for teachers to keep track of.

When I'm helping a gallery curator friend write a press release for an exhibit of art by mothers—all of whom, including me, are women—and she sheepishly suggests we omit the word "woman," I don't object. Like her, I understand that to claim my native womanhood as something at all distinguishable from trans-womanhood—and my motherhood as something inseverable from my womanhood—is to risk being branded a "transphobe" or "TERF," no matter how fully I support trans rights.

I should not mention to anyone outside my closest circle my discomfort reading the *Self* magazine story titled "Six Things You Should Know Before Having Top Surgery," as if it were dishing out tips for a kettlebell workout.

When the third mother in a two-month span tells me that her own teenage child has had, or will be having, top surgery—which is another way of saying they have had, or will be having, their breasts removed—I respond with a gentle head tilt and support-ive nod. I do not let on, as I am nodding, the visceral sorrow this image has stirred in me; my mind struggles to disentangle it from all the violences perpetrated on the bodies of girls—and which girls, far too often, turn on themselves. Nodding at this mother, I wonder for an instant if I might have had my breasts removed had this option been commonly available when I was in the throes of adolescence, the new and unruly markers of my femaleness filling me with such humiliation that I starved myself down to an amenorrheic androgyny. I knew nothing at all, in those days, of the powers lying dormant in my breasts—the pleasure of them cupped in the hands of a lover, the miracle of them nourishing new life.

I keep these thoughts silent, too—not just now, but always. I keep silent as I watch my daughter out of the corner of my eye, my reservations building in me like a sinister subplot.

I don't know what to say when Leigh is greeted as a boy, for I haven't figured out what to do with my uncertainty, or what kind of mother to be in this upside-down theater. And so I say nothing as we leave Starbucks, nothing on the far side of the crosswalk, nothing after we've passed the temple security guard—because to say *something* feels like stepping into a thicket I don't know how to beat a path through. To say something is to name, and to name is to turn the intangible into something real and solid and corporeal that must be reckoned with.

One day, without warning, Paul steps right into this thicket. Our family has just arrived at a tropical-themed family party at a restaurant, where a smiling waiter distributes leis of orchids to the female guests, and cowrie bead necklaces to the male ones. As Leigh pulls the beads she's been handed over her head, Paul turns to her: "Do you want us to say anything," he asks, "when they assume you're a boy?" My breath catches behind my ribs. From where I stand, ruminating and paralyzed, even this simple question seems reckless. Leigh is quiet for a moment, and then she shrugs a little.

"I guess I don't really care either way," she says.

It makes sense that Paul, a less tentative human than me generally, would be less tentative about entering this territory. But I wonder, sometimes, if his comparative ease when we discuss the changes in Leigh behind closed doors has anything to do with the fact that the version of selfhood our daughter is migrating toward is *his* version of selfhood, original and familiar to him. Every day that passes feels like one more mile she's drifted from me, her native homeland, to a foreign harbor. There's pain for me in this parting, a pain it's difficult for me to give voice to, though I hear it, from time to time, in my barbed attempts at lightness. "If she is going to dress like a guy," I say to Paul one day after Leigh leaves the house in a Hawaiian shirt and chinos, "must it be a middle-aged insurance salesman?" A little gallows humor to temper my grief.

Maybe, in this way, my story isn't a new story, though its details are particular to our era. Maybe it's the story shared by parents everywhere, for time immemorial, who've had to accept, as their children grow, that they are not them. Maybe I've reached that turning point all parents, in their individual ways, must someday reach, when the world, it feels, has spun out from under our feet, taking our children with it toward a future we can't catch up to.

One spring afternoon, I pick up Leigh at school, and she slides into the passenger seat beside me. She opens a bag of potato chips and fiddles with the radio buttons, stopping when she gets to KISS FM. Dove Cameron's "Boyfriend" is on again. *I could be a better boyfriend than him*, crows Cameron in her sultry soprano to the implied female love interest she's trying to steal. Leigh hums and bops along with her shoulders for a bit, and then pauses: "Just pretend you don't notice the bad language, Mom," she says.

"What bad language?"

"You didn't hear that?"

I listen closer. "Beyond the boyfriend part I can barely make out the words."

"Huh," Leigh says. She crunches a potato chip, takes a sip from her water bottle. "Maybe it's like how there are certain frequencies people can't hear anymore once they're old," she jokes.

Maybe so, I think, as we speed through stands of oak trees thickening with leaves—for I am no longer certain whether my years allow me to see more than my oldest child, or whether they keep me from seeing the things she sees at all.

ACT V

As far as I know, Rosalind is the only Shakespearean character ever to be the subject of a biography. On the surface, this concept makes no sense at all, since biographies are about real, not made up, people. But theater scholar Angela Thirlwell pulls the conceit off beautifully in *Rosalind: Shakespeare's Immortal Heroine*, which I discover one afternoon at my town library. From the moment I could read, my favorite characters have often felt more real to me than living people—and here, according to the flap copy, was someone as taken by Rosalind as I was.

In bed that night, I skip ahead to the chapter "Call Me Ganymede—Rosalind Crosses the Border," hoping, as my daughter drifts into her own borderlands across the hall, it might contain something helpful. As I read, I'm reminded that, in Shakespeare's time, male actors performed all female roles, since women were barred from the stage. This means that by the middle of *As You Like It*, Rosalind contains not two or even three but *four* layers of gender: She's a man (the actor), who plays a woman (Rosalind),

who is pretending to be a man (Ganymede), who then impersonates a woman (Rosalind). You'd think all this switching back and
forth would confuse audiences. But as I think back to the pro-
ductions of the play I've seen—from that outdoor staging on the
Boston Common, to the BBC film version with Helen Mirren, to
the Kenneth Branagh adaptation set in Japan—I can't remember
ever losing grasp of which Rosalind I was watching. Or, more
accurately, it didn't so much *matter* which Rosalind I was watching, because her layers had melded into a single, cohesive character, whose moods and fluctuations made perfect sense. At one
moment, this character might be more masculine, and at another
more feminine—but she was always, always Rosalind.

In my first teaching job, in my twenties, I co-taught eleventh
grade English with another new teacher, who would become one
of the most treasured friends of my life. Sara and I pored over
Catch-22 and *The Color Purple* together, planned lessons after
school together, and graded essays over sangria together, becoming, over time, such a constant and mutually adoring unit that
another teacher, Brian, took to calling us the Married Couple. In
the faculty room one day, he posed to us a very heteronormative
and possibly flirtatious question: "So, which one of you is the husband, and which one the wife?"

It was a puzzle that depended entirely on superficial gender
stereotypes—and therefore a puzzle unworthy of being solved.
And yet, against our better judgment, we found ourselves thinking
about it. I'm more demure than Sara, we decided, but also more
practical. Sara is bolder than I am, but also more emotional. I'm
daintier than Sara, but also more thick-skinned. She's sturdier than
I am, but also more porous. No matter how many times we went
over it, the traits culturally marked as "male" and "female" seemed

to exist in us more or less equally—just as they do in the rational, irrational, sensible, romantic, courageous, and cautious Rosalind, whose power lies not, I've come to believe, in her assumption of maleness, but in her ability to transcend the categories of gender altogether.

When I'm with Leigh and we run into people we haven't seen in a while, I can see how they struggle with her in-betweenness. Their eyes stay on her a second too long; their weight shifts. *What is she?* they seem to be thinking. I'm as susceptible to the urge to classify as anyone, but I've begun to notice, in these moments, a protective impulse flare in me. *Step back,* I want to warn them. *Leave her be.* I cannot tell these people what my daughter *is*: When I look at her, in this moment, I see only my child.

On the last day of sixth grade, I take Leigh for lunch to celebrate. The sun shines on our outside table, and while I haven't planned to have a Serious Talk about Identity with her, something about the gentle air of this day prompts me to dip a toe in. I mention a child at Leigh's Hebrew school who has started going by "they/them" pronouns, marveling aloud at how far the world has come since I was her age, at how much more sophisticatedly her generation thinks about gender. Leigh's eyes dance; her whole body seems to buzz to life. And then she begins to talk to me— volubly and gleefully, like an eager scholar—about all she knows and feels and thinks on this subject.

A silence opens up. "Leigh," I say, smoothing out the napkin on my lap, "I've been curious how *you* think about your gender."

She looks at me, surprised and a little delighted. She smiles a bit. She thinks for a moment. And then she claps her head in her hands in a pantomime of confusion. "I don't know!" she says. "I never know what to say when teachers ask us to go around and say what our pronouns are."

She falls quiet and circles her spoon in her pasta. I can see she has said all she will.

Before I know it, I am articulating things to my daughter that I haven't, until this very moment, known I've thought. Things about how rapidly the world is moving, and how insistently it seems to want its children to catch up. Things about the beauty and truth that can bloom in the taking of time. Leigh listens, almost certainly not fully understanding my ramblings, but happily spooning up her pasta nonetheless, and then after a while we drift to another topic, and she orders another Sprite, and I eat another piece of bread. From the outside it looks like nothing at this table has changed, but on this dappled patio of the Cheesecake Factory, there's a lightness between us I haven't felt in ages.

As You Like It is very much a play about lightness. When its characters flee the court, they trade rigidity and convention for open-endedness and improvisation: in Arden's pastures, they can follow their curiosities, test out alternatives, reverse course, live "as they like." This flexibility is what separates Shakespeare's comic heroes from his tragic ones—like Lear, or Macbeth, or Othello, whose single-minded need for certainty sends them hurtling toward death, the ultimate final conclusion. I remember being totally fascinated to learn, from my college Shakespeare professor, that the conditional word "if" appears more often in *As You Like It* than in any other Shakespeare play—nearly a hundred and fifty times. Most of these appearances occur while the characters are in Arden, its spirit of possibility alive even at the sentence level. Touchstone, the court clown who's tagged along with Rosalind and Celia to the forest, delivers a lengthy ode to the swinging-door magic of this little conjunction, which can make anything provisional. "Your If is the only peacemaker," he proclaims. "Much virtue in If."

Much virtue in If. I've been returning to this phrase lately, revolving it in my mind, holding it up as a sort of mantra. So often, as a mother, I'm either being a gatekeeper, barring my children from going where I feel they shouldn't, or a cheerleader, speeding them to where I feel they should. But between these poles lies another way—which is to be Arden, a neutral witness to my children's wanderings, a shaded wood where they can play out their possible selves. It isn't easy for me to linger in semidarkness. Maybe it's hard for all of us. We want our clear outlines, our firm contours. We want our drawers and our shelves, our slots and compartments. We want our ten steps, our seven stages, our five acts, our three acts. We want our introductions and conclusions—and here, before I bid adieu, is mine:

That night, before she goes to sleep, Leigh calls to me from her room: "You coming, Mom?" I'm certain that, any day now, she'll decide she's too old for this ritual, and I'll be dispatched for good. But for now, I'm still wanted here, on this bed cluttered with stuffed animals, under a poster of Harry Styles—a perfectly composed tableau of human becoming. I curl my arm around my daughter, tucking it under her side. As we lie in the quiet, I think for a second that I should probably seize this opportunity to pick up our conversation from lunch, probe a bit more, help Leigh get to the bottom of what it is she is and how she wants to be seen.

Is loving the same thing as seeing? In this moment, I feel that it's not.

I reach out across the chasm of my blindness, taking my child's hand in the dark.

The Friendship Plot

I f this were a love story, I would start by describing the rain. A June midafternoon downpour, the sky an overturned trough. I would recall my drenched pants, the ones with the creases that my mother had bought me for interviews, slapping across my ankles as I walked from the subway. I'd recall cursing my failed umbrella, and how my feet slid around in my shoes as I entered the school's lobby.

On a bench by the door sat a woman around my age. She smiled at me and I forced a smile back as my pants dripped water on the carpet. Her smile didn't stop, though. It kept going—lips, cheeks, eyes—gathering energy the way a smile does when it can't be helped. It was a smile that made me feel a little less soaked, or maybe that it was perfectly normal that I'd arrived here soaked, for really, wasn't everyone, under their most professional clothes, a damp, matted down, trembling, very small thing?

The only other seat in the room was next to her. I could feel her eying me gently as I settled in, and then she leaned my way. "Are you here for an interview?" she whispered. How did she know? And wasn't this violating some sort of protocol, this breaking of the reception area fourth wall? This tiny subversion thrilled me, the way it turned us in an instant into confidantes.

"I am," I said.

"Same!" she said.

Was she science? Or history? She looked more history than science, with her trumpet skirt and bouclé sweater, her hair pinned in loose twists with butterfly clips in a way I'd sometimes attempted to arrange mine. "For an English position," she added, and I realized that I'd met my competition.

But wait, not competition, because a moment later, a pair of doors opened and out bounded the head of school, thick-browed and grinning. "Wonderful!" he said. "I see you two have met," and he ushered us, puzzled, into his office. We sat before his desk in matching armchairs, and he explained—or not explained, more like *pronounced*, as if officiating a wedding—his plan for us. He was impressed by our resumes! And wished he could hire us both! But since there was only one open position, what we must naturally do was share it: two sections of eleventh grade literature for each of us until another opening arose. He scribbled on a piece of paper and pushed it across his desk. Together, we beheld our mutual salaries, surprisingly high for part-time.

He slapped his desk with finality. "What do you say?"

I turned to the stranger beside me, truly seeing her face for the very first time. Pale eyes, magisterial cheekbones. She looked, at once, both young and ancient, like a maiden cast in marble. He saw something in her—in me, in *us*—this man offering us a job without bothering to ask us a single question. I wanted very much to know what it was.

I opened my palms, inviting in her answer, and she responded with her eyes, a quick bright flash of decision.

"Yes," I said.

"Yes," she said.

And so our story began.

. . .

My children love to hear the tale of when their dad and I met. They never tire of the details: how despite being a total homebody, I was overcome that evening by a peculiar urge to *socialize*; how we'd ended up at the same weird party at the Puck Building in Soho, where circus performers roamed the room swallowing fire; how we started making small talk by the bar, and then talked to no one else until one a.m.; how Paul was mortified, when he asked for my number, that he'd forgotten my name, and so cleverly handed me his phone to create my own contact.

My own parents met on a blind date at Martell's-by-the-Sea in Amagansett, Long Island, a moment memorialized by a framed restaurant poster on our hallway wall. When I was little, it wasn't just the romance of this story that thrilled me but its wildly high stakes, those stakes being my existence. My kids, too, like to ponder how narrowly they skirted oblivion. "What if you hadn't gone to that party?" they say. "What if Daddy had left before you arrived?" Then we would not be sitting here, in this rowhouse flanked by rhododendrons, at a breakfast table dappled with marker stains, enjoying crepes with whipped cream while Leigh reads aloud from the funnies. There would be no Leigh at all, of course. And no Jacob, perpetually getting out of his seat to do a head spin. And no Nora, humming while she chews. This prospect fills me with a gratitude so huge it verges on panic.

Courtship, romance, a wedding, the ever-after—Paul's and my story adheres neatly to the classic marriage plot. Its denouement is always right here in front of us: in these children we made, this home we created, these photos and books and dishes and pets and rugs and treasures we've amassed. No one would have to squint to understand what we mean to each other. Our entire lives are a semaphore of our love.

The nature of a friendship is harder to discern. There are no vows to define it or rings to formalize it. It needs no house to contain it or papers to certify it. Its scope cannot be grasped with the naked eye.

I'll show you a few snapshots of me and Sara, the stranger who careened into my life just months after Paul. Here we are at twenty-four, eating hummus and red pepper sandwiches on the bench across the street from our school. Here we are at twenty-nine, on a beach in the Outer Banks with Paul and Phil. Here we are at thirty-five, shooing our kids off to play while we chat on her porch. Here we are at forty-three, talking on Zoom from our kitchens in different time zones. *Friends*, you might look at us and say. *Girlfriends*, you might say. *BFFs* you might say, though I really hope you wouldn't. There's no precise word in our language for what we are to each other; they are all cuter and lesser than the truth.

I think back often to that rainy afternoon twenty years ago, when we were implausibly hired as co-teachers without any experience. What if I hadn't decided to leave my editorial assistant job? What if she'd stuck it out in production at ABC News? What if my resumé had ended up in the head of school's spam folder? What if she'd woken up that day with the flu?

Well then, I wouldn't exist. There would be someone walking around who looked like me, with the same fingerprints as me, and the same chromosomes as me, but she would not be me. She would be smaller, duller, meaner. I can tell you with near certainty I wouldn't like her.

. . .

September came. We printed our class lists and blundered our way through creating a shared syllabus. We had no idea what we were doing—mutual imposters trying to play it cool.

After school, we started meeting in the faculty room to pore over *Frankenstein*, as if dissecting each sentence we'd assigned could make us good teachers. I had my first glimpse, in those hours, of the power of Sara's mind: the sideways leaps it made; the way it grasped, in just a few words, what I was trying to say. But it wasn't her intelligence, exactly, that made these meetings feel like something bigger than a planning session. It was her intelligence mixed with her fanatical love for Bologna, where she'd briefly lived; her intelligence mixed with the way her laughter came from a place so deep you could hardly hear it. I felt drawn to her as you might an unusual stone, or a familiar melody transposed to a minor key.

I noticed that she seemed to have more time than most people, as if surrounded by an invisible cushion of extra minutes. This was very interesting. I'd be scrambling down the hall to my sixth period class—clutching a warm stack of photocopies, shoving the last bite of a bagel in my mouth—and there she'd be outside her classroom, chatting in Italian with Dr. Abdullah, the world languages chair, or listening to our department head rhapsodize about Jack Kerouac again. She seemed to trust that the pieces of her day would somehow fall into place—and as far as I could tell, they more or less always did.

About a month into the school year, I passed Sara's classroom after last period. The door was open, and her class was cleaning up after some sort of celebration. She swept through the room with a trash basket, depositing cups and crumpled napkins, and then paused before one of her students.

"Are you going to eat that?" she said, pointing to the triangle of pizza on her plate.

"Nope," her student said.

And do you want to know what she did next? She picked up that pizza and took a tremendous bite of it. She laughed a little as she did this, and her student laughed too. This all happened in an instant, as if it were nothing. But to me, it was far from nothing. It was the seed of a riveting philosophical question. Could a person take a bite of her student's pizza? One could indeed, for Sara had. And this meant that I—if I wanted to do such a thing—could, too.

For the girl I'd been and the woman I newly was—acutely attuned to life's unspoken rules, partially numbed by years of behaving as expected—this was a powerful discovery. It revealed to me just how fragile the membrane is between the ordinary and the interesting. At any moment, I realized, I could poke my finger through the flimsy casing around me, and things could be otherwise.

Maybe all friendships begin with fascination. Maybe we discover, in those who transfix us, clues to the person we're aching to become.

My mother didn't spend much time with friends when I was young. There were ladies she had coffee with on occasion, this or that mother of one of our classmates. But these relationships were always peripheral and invisible, something that happened outside the frame of our real lives. Mostly, her social life revolved around my father, whose social life revolved around work: restaurant dinners with his clients and their wives, or holiday gatherings with his partners and their families. "A wife ought not to have friends of her own but ought to share those of her husband," wrote Plutarch, two thousand years ago, in his *Precepts on Marriage*. No one, certainly, would have made such a statement in our household; but in practice, its spirit was very much alive.

For most of Western history, deep fellowship was considered the province of men. Nearly all written accounts of friendship before the seventh century center on male bonds, which were deemed vital for civil and military cohesion, while women were dismissed by Aristotle, Cicero, and other classical philosophers as unequipped for the loyalty and sacrifice of true friendship. In the Middle Ages, the Christian convent emerged as a space for women to commune with other women outside of their families. But even here, only a generalized camaraderie was encouraged; *particular* friendships were prohibited, lest they weaken the nuns' singular devotion to God.

Close bonds between unrelated women grew more common and visible in the late 1500s. In England, one observer described how well-to-do wives spent time "visiting their friends and keeping company, conversing with their equals" and "making merry with them"—and all, he added, "with the permission of their husbands as such is the custom." Female friendships blossomed in literature around this time as well, most notably in the works of Shakespeare, who created some of the most iconic female duos in the Western canon: not just Rosalind and Celia, but also Desdemona and Emilia, Beatrice and Hero, and Hermia and Helena. This last pair were as attached to each other in girlhood as "two lovely berries molded on one stem / So with two seeming bodies but one heart." I loved this image in seventh grade, when my English teacher Ms. Schwartz used it to explain what a simile was, and I knew exactly what Shakespeare meant by it, because when my best friend Katie was upset, I could feel it behind my ribs. I didn't understand why Helena and Hermia had to start threatening to scratch each other's eyes out over Lysander. And while the end of *A Midsummer Night's Dream*, with its big triple wedding, was okay, it left me with a sort of wistful nostalgia for things as they'd been.

But this, I would come to learn, is what the marriage plot calls for: a turn from friendship toward heterosexual romance, a redirection of the heroine's affections. The female bond in this story arc becomes secondary—a mere "rehearsal in girlhood," as Henry Wadsworth Longfellow put it in his 1849 novel *Kavanagh*, "of the great drama of woman's life": marriage and family. Without this reorientation, whether in Shakespeare's plays or Hollywood romcoms, there's no correction of misunderstanding, no ordering of chaos, no balance restored. The happy ending depends on it.

I sometimes wonder if my parents' marriage would have gone differently had my mother had a few close friends. Or even just one good friend, steady and true. Maybe then she wouldn't have seemed, always, to be slightly bewildered by her life, as if she were in one of those dreams where you find yourself standing on a stage unclear what you're there for. Maybe her friend could have been like a mirror to her, helping her remember the fullness of who she was, or like a lantern, casting light on all she might still become. Maybe then, she wouldn't have needed to demolish the whole stage to get off it.

In the quiet Connecticut town where my mother now lives, she has three close friends. They have breakfast together every

Wednesday at the Village Market, and if I were to accidentally call her cellphone while she was there, I'm not sure she'd answer. She laughs often, and has that hard-to-rattle quality of someone who understands who she is.

It's hard to know when fascination blooms into friendship. Was it the afternoon Sara and I moved our planning sessions down the street to Café con Leche, lingering for hours over plates of oily tostones? Or the day my jeans got muddy on a field trip and she magically handed me a fresh pair of sweatpants from her bag. Or was it the first time we got together with our fiancés, the four of us testing our chemistry over a pot of bubbling fondue. I became conscious, with Paul and Phil there making small talk over their beef skewers, of how activated we became in each other's presence, like two plucked guitar strings, all vibration and reverb.

It was, by any traditional measure, an exciting year for the two of us: both set to be married in a matter of months, both freshly astonished to be accelerating toward the happily-ever-after portion of our lives. But this thing between us, too, was a kind of romance, with its own breathless thrill, its own private language of affection. No one before had commented on the dignity of my posture as I sat at a computer, or marveled at how completely my handwriting captured my essence. I had not known, until she mentioned it, that I had an essence, let alone one worthy of being transmitted to paper.

For her birthday that winter, I wrote her a sonnet. For no particular occasion that spring, I crocheted her a scarf. Never before had I been inspired to write someone a sonnet. Never before had I wanted to make anyone a scarf.

We laughed constantly, our laughter merging between us like a song in stereo. We laughed, especially, at times when laughter was inappropriate, clamping our hands over our mouths during professional development meetings, slinking down in our seats during Cum Laude award assemblies. The things we found funny tended toward the absurd, like the time we used a stale fruitcake a parent had regifted me as a volleyball at the faculty holiday party, or the time she hid—and in the nick of time produced—my copy of *Crime and Punishment* right before class. *Crime and Punishment* was a serious and profound and daunting book to teach—but also an excellent prop for a practical joke.

The summer after our first year of teaching, we attended a conference together at an International Baccalaureate high school in New Mexico. After long morning sessions, we would step out of the air-conditioned library onto a sunny courtyard shared by the school's working farm, with its corral of friendly alpacas. They were a sight to see, these alpacas, blithely munching hay in the middle of campus. But on the other hand, it was lunchtime. While she stood beside me murmuring *Look at those eyes! Look at that fluff!*, I silently imagined how long the cafeteria line was getting. It was, and still is, like this with her at times, the extremes of her wonder stretching me to the edges of my patience. But when I look back on that week now, what I remember above all are those creatures: the prick of their ears in the heat, the burst of their fur between my fingers.

And I remember this. On the final evening of the conference, at a picnic table under a purpling sky, we revealed to each other the most shameful thing we'd ever done, the thing about us nearly no one knew. It doesn't matter what she shared with me, or what I shared with her. What matters is what she told me after, as we walked the moonlit pathway back to the dorm. "It means so much to me," she said, "that I can tell you anything and trust that you won't be shocked."

Was this true? Possibly it was. But it was also possible that it was *she* who had made me this way, spacious enough to admit life's darkest shadows.

We become ourselves, in part, through the women we befriend. They imagine us a little better than we are, and what they picture comes true.

I think there should be more movies about the transformative magic of female friendship, epics with sweeping landscapes and orchestral soundtracks. I first had this thought a few weeks ago, while watching the movie *Mean Girls* with Leigh, who couldn't get over the fact that I'd never seen it. She warned me that it contained some "inappropriate" moments, and so I'd settled onto the couch with a bowl of popcorn, prepared to be cringingly entertained.

Instead, between occasional funny parts, I was bored. While Rachel McAdams's character spread rumors about Lindsey Lohan's character, and Lindsey Lohan's character ridiculed Amanda Seyfried's character, and Amanda Seyfried's character backstabbed Rachel McAdams's character, I stole glances at my email behind a throw pillow. The problem was that I'd seen this story so many times before—not this exact story, with this exact script, but ones with the same basic message: that girls and women are wired for rivalry, and the bonds between us can't be trusted. When I was Leigh's age, I learned this from *Heathers* and *Beverly Hills, 90210*; in my twenties, from *Clueless* and *Cruel Intentions*; and in the decades since, from every reality TV show with the word "Housewives" or "Bride" in the title.

A year ago, for five upsetting minutes, I thought Leigh might be a "mean girl." The reason I thought this was because the director of her sleepaway camp was on the phone from Maine telling me as much. He reported that she and three girls from her bunk had formed a clique, and other girls were getting left out. A behavior contract had been drawn up. "I sat them down and explained to them," he told me matter-of-factly, "that I won't put up with any of that mean girl stuff here."

My first reaction was shock, because while Leigh certainly isn't perfect, treating others kindly has never been her particular challenge. I pressed the director for examples of her meanness. Was she bullying other campers? *No*, he said. Was she mocking them, saying cruel things to them, or talking about them behind their backs? *No*, he said. In the end, the only data he could provide was that Leigh and these three girls were constantly together, and that they wore their baseball hats backward, and that they called each other by funny insider names.

I can see how funny insider names go against the "one for all and all for one" spirit of summer camp—really, I can. But there's a vast difference between holding tight to the people you adore and maliciously excluding others. This difference should be obvious. But it occurred to me later that night, as I lay in bed realizing I had a right to feel angry, how often these things are conflated when it comes to girls. The very word "clique," with its negative connotations, is a gendered word—like "coven." *A coven of witches. A clique of girls.* Female alliances have a long, precarious history of being twisted into something sinister.

Jacob has two best friends. They spend every recess together doing yo-yo tricks, they sit together at every lunch, and they have lots of insider jokes—but no one has ever described them to me as a "clique" or accused them of being "mean boys." They are best buds, partners in crime, the three musketeers.

I can imagine, in a different world—one less threatened by what can brew inside a circle of women—receiving another sort of call from my daughter's camp director. *I have some good news!* he might say. *Leigh has formed deep friendships with three girls in particular. She's experiencing what it means to choose and be chosen, to know and be known. It's a beautiful thing to see.*

I have an encyclopedic knowledge, at this point, of Sara. She was born in Indiana, moved to North Carolina when she was three, then moved back to Indiana when she was nine. She has a B.A. in English from Notre Dame and an M.A. in English from CUNY. Her father is an ER doctor and her mother a homemaker. Her younger brother is a chemical engineer who invented something important I'm not equipped to explain. She was raised Catholic but has one Jewish grandmother on her father's side. We make much of this Jewish grandmother, as if she were the ancestral spool from which the thread that binds us unwinds.

She's the niece of four aunts and two uncles. She's an aunt to one niece and one nephew. She is the mother of one bright and gentle son, Sam, whom I held in my arms at St. Mary's Hospital in Hoboken, New Jersey, when he was one day old, and who is now a few months away from heading to college.

The most important teacher of her life was Mr. Zwerneman, her eleventh grade humanities instructor, who made her believe her ideas might actually matter. Her favorite candy is Runts. Her favorite sandwich is a Reuben. Her favorite animal is a dolphin. She is happiest by a body of saltwater with a vigorous breeze on her skin.

She's a Capricorn, a tooth grinder, a passionate drinker of seltzer. She is prone to bronchitis and allergic to stone fruits. Visually, she's a cross between the actor Rachel Weisz and a peony.

In middle school, she started taking fencing lessons. In high school, she fenced. In college, she fenced. She fenced so often and so wholeheartedly that she eventually won three NCAA championship medals and was the women's foil alternate at the 1996 Olympic Games in Atlanta. This is absolutely true. And remarkable! And yet I often forget about it, because it isn't one of the top ten things I appreciate about her. It isn't even in the top one hundred—except in the way her devotion to the things she loves makes vivid all there is in the world to love. Except in the way that being with her can feel like a back-and-forth dance on a fencing strip, each of us alive to the other's thoughts, advancing and retreating, predicting and parrying.

It's hard, when I speak of her, to stick to the facts. The biographical keeps giving way to the ineffable.

Maybe this is what true friendship always does: tunnels straight past the achievements and failures that define us, the stories that cling to us like clothes we've fallen asleep in. The sixteenth-century philosopher Michel de Montaigne, in his essay "On Friendship," distinguishes between common "ordinary" friendship, which always carries a whiff of the transactional, and true friendship, which has no other purpose than itself. The great true friend of Montaigne's lifetime was the writer Étienne de la Boétie, about whom he reveals very little in his essay except that it's as if they share a soul. And this, in the end, may be all we need to know. "If a man should importune me to give reason why I loved him," Montaigne tells us, "I find it could no otherwise be expressed than by making answer: because it was he, because it was I."

There are endless itemizable reasons, when you're a woman, why others might value you. Because you're agreeable, because you smile easily, because you're game. Because you're pretty, have shiny hair, have a nice ass. Because you know exactly what questions to ask to make your conversation partner feel they are fascinating. Because you'd make a good wife, or good mother, or good PTO volunteer. Because you're funny, but not bitingly funny. Because you're smart, but not pedantically smart. Because you give excellent presents, or excellent advice, or excellent head.

I love my husband through and through. I love his steady mind, his quick sense of humor, his spirit of celebration. I love how we've grown together like two entwined branches, yielding and bending to support each other's becoming. I love that, after more than two decades together, I am still caught off guard at times by how handsome I find him.

But I wonder sometimes if marriage, with its contractual origins, can ever fully transcend the transactional. In a marriage, it can feel as if something is always owed, because it's entirely impossible, despite the gauzy hopes we pin on matrimony, for two people to fulfill each other's every need. And so shadowing Paul's and my love—shadowing *all* marital love, perhaps—are the ways in which we suspect we are falling short, or getting shorted. It isn't his fault, or my fault, that our relationship seems to consist of so much *tallying*—of who is or isn't giving the other enough attention, or praise, or hope, or space, or comfort, or sex. No matter how sound a marriage is at its core, it is always, inevitably, haunted by its own illusory standards.

For us striving wives and mothers of the world, worn out from the exertions of trying to conform to a dream, female friendship might be the only place where we can simply be. Inside our cliques of two, there's no script to follow, no end of the bargain to hold up, no proof to produce, again and again, that we are worthy. All that matters, in this quiet sanctuary, is that she is she. All that matters, in this sacred temple, is that you are you.

Do I need to clarify that I don't love Sara *that* way? The mind so often leaps to the erotic when we talk about intimacy—a conditioned reflex, I assume, of living in a culture that prizes romantic love over other forms of affection.

For centuries, across cultures, great thinkers have tried to make the case for platonic love. Plato argued that friendship—what the ancient Greeks called *philia*—is the highest form of human connection *because* it requires no physical attraction. In the Celtic tradition, the *anam cara*, or "soul friend," has long been considered a vital element of human unfolding. The Buddha, when asked by his own friend Ananda whether friendship has a place in the spiritual life, declared that it is in fact "the *whole* of the spiritual life." And yet, there's something in us that loves to suspect the platonic of being "more" than platonic, that yearns to find in it a sexual through line burning its way toward a combustive and satisfying end.

In the Hebrew bible, sexual intercourse is often referred to by a form of the root *yada*, which means "to know." When we're told that Adam *knew* his wife Eve, and she conceived Cain—or that Cain *knew* his own wife, and she conceived Enoch—the word "know" is being used euphemistically. But in its own subtle and lovely way, it also points to the elements of intimacy that are cognitive rather than carnal: attending, perceiving, understanding, recognizing, allowing. *Yada*, in Hebrew, also means to grasp something to the depths of its being. Our spouses and lovers might have this sort of knowledge of us—but so, too, do our most treasured friends.

And yet, even as I make this distinction between the erotic and the platonic, it occurs to me that the deep knowing of friendship might be its own sort of physical union. It's the melding of bodies I experience when I hear one of Sara's expressions tumble from my lips, or when my eyebrow spontaneously rises exactly like hers. It's the plug-and-socket fusion of brain circuitry I feel when I finish one of her sentences, or when she explains to me, because I just can't figure it out, why that thing my father said yesterday left me feeling so sad. We have grown, over the years, into a more complete version of what we were hired to be from the start: one teacher, and one woman, in two bodies.

Not long ago, a therapist friend told me that it's common for her straight, married, women patients to admit to her "somewhat sheepishly" that while they love their husbands—of course, of course!—it's with their female friends that they've experienced the greatest intimacy. This didn't surprise me one bit. I can't imagine it would surprise most women I know. And yet I, too, I realized, have tiptoed around a little "sheepishly" with this knowledge, as if by communing so nakedly with my closest women friends I am cheating on…who exactly? Not so much Paul, but the fundamental premise of what it means to be married.

Here, for the world to know, is the barely hidden secret of us heterosexual ladies with our wedding bands and anniversary trips and date nights and glowing monogamous devotion to the men we married: wrapped tenderly and snugly around our hearts, like an invisible ring, is our love of another woman. Or two. Or more.

My favorite photo from Paul's and my wedding isn't one of the soft-focus portraits captured by our photographer, but a blurry snapshot taken by one of our guests. It's late in the night—my skin shines through my makeup, and wisps of hair fall from my chignon. Paul and I are dancing, his right hand pressed to my lower back, my left hand draped across his elbow. It would be a pretty run-of-the-mill wedding composition, were it not for the fact that Sara is in the frame as well, holding tight with two hands to my other wrist, trying to pull me away to dance with her, goddammit. Paul is grinning in mock disbelief at me, and I am grinning fiendishly at her, our tug-of-war triangle its own sort of dance.

Over the years, Paul has teased Sara about this moment—how even on our *wedding night*, she tried to steal me from him. It's a joke made with affection; but in humor, truth, they say. My husband knows, though we do not speak of it, that my philia lover will always have access to parts of me that he doesn't, that our friendship is an affair of the heart committed over and over.

If I were a fiction writer, I might use that dancefloor snapshot as inspiration for a page-turning story. It would be a tale of rivalry, about a husband and a best friend vying for the heroine's affections. Tensions would simmer toward a climactic standoff, in which the best friend wrests the heroine from her husband's arms on their wedding night, luring her outside for some "fresh air," where a get-away car awaits, engine idling, to whisk them away.

But since this is a true story, I'll tell you what really happened after that photo was taken. My best friend pulled me away, spinning off with me across the dancefloor—her silver dress flashing, my tulle gown swirling—and then spun me back into my husband's arms, where I realized with a shiver of surprise that it is, in fact, possible to feel entirely happy and at peace. In this version of the story, the best friend isn't a villain, or an obstacle, or a temporary stepping stone. She's the arc that completes the whole.

This friendship plot, as we have lived it, has no climax of *any* sort, in fact. There are no showdowns or sudden illnesses, no moment when Sara betrays me and I must learn to trust her again, no point at which I fail her, and she must learn to forgive me.

We all know that a story should have a climax. I taught my own students this, year after year, diagraming the components of narrative structure on the whiteboard using Freytag's Pyramid: exposition, rising action, climax, falling action, resolution. (This pyramid, importantly, could just as easily be used to diagram sex—or rather, a male-centric idea of sex: forward-driving, linear, building toward a singular explosion before plummeting back to baseline, spent and satisfied.)

But in the twenty years we've been friends, there have been no conflicts between Sara and me—only shared obstacles. There's been the geographical challenge, since I moved to Boston, of staying close across hundreds of miles. There has been the challenge of my subsumption, each time I've given birth to another child, into the moment-to-moment demands of early motherhood. And there's been the unbearable space between us when depression has pulled her, once again, into its undertow, and her spirit is like a coin I search for below fathoms of water.

Our friendship plot, as you can see, is an essentially happy plot. But is it attention-grabbing? Does it have "bite," as my undergraduate writing professor used to call that intangible something that keeps readers turning the pages?

If I were to diagram our story with a dry-erase marker, what would it look like? Maybe a winding path that rises and dips, like a gentle stroll over grassy hills. Or the spiral of a snail's shell, widening as it circles out from its center.

Or perhaps it would just be a line, sloping upward from one corner of the board to the other. It would need no tension to keep it going, this line, just the steady fuel of mutual care and devotion. Up and off the whiteboard it would climb, streaking across the sky until the ink runs dry.

Very Nice Blastocysts

The photograph is in a file box in our attic, the one full of things I'll never discard: the first note my husband ever scrawled to me, a swatch from my wedding dress, a wine-ringed napkin from our honeymoon, the deed to our house.

In the photo, two gray circles float against a darker gray backdrop. Within each circle are eight smaller circles, clustered like bubbles. The bubbles are cells, and the circles, embryos—*our* embryos, Paul's and mine—cajoled into existence seven years ago.

When I first saw this photo, I sat naked from the waist down, covered in a paper sheet, moments away from the embryo transfer I prayed would result in a second child and more family of my own to nurture to make up for the broken one I came from. With our daughter Leigh, medication alone had solved the problem of my long-ago diagnosed "unexplained infertility," pulling us back from the brink of IVF. This time, we weren't so lucky.

But hope was not lost. These were promising embryos, said Dr. Carter, our reproductive endocrinologist—the best sort of embryos, which are graded on a numbered scale, like diamonds. Our embryos were beautiful, grade-one diamonds, their cut and clarity excellent, the cells even, the cytoplasm lucid and free of fragments. I stared at them, swelling with a pride that was already, in its way, maternal.

With my feet in stirrups, I watched Dr. Carter pick up the loaded catheter. Centimeter-by-centimeter, she ferried our embryos up through the caverns of my body, past my cervix, into my womb, where she released them, gently, meticulously—the fish slipped back into the river—to forces beyond her control.

Science, through the hormones I'd injected nightly into my stomach, could stimulate my ovaries to make eggs. With a needle and suction tube, it could extract these eggs. With a high-speed centrifuge, it could separate out my husband's choicest sperm, and then mix these with my eggs in a petri dish. It could, through progesterone supplements, thicken the lining of my uterus, laying a rich bed for the resulting embryos. It could determine, based on my age and an algorithm, how many embryos to transfer to maximize our odds of a baby while minimizing our odds of multiple babies. But here, science fell powerless, for it has never found a way to make an embryo take root in a woman's body.

"You can stay lying down for ten minutes," Dr. Carter said before leaving the room. I stayed for an hour, the pressure on my tailbone mounting. I closed my eyes and sank deep into myself, as if I could will my womb to latch on to one of those floating circles. I stayed until my edges dissolved, until I felt I was nothing but a snug bed of soil, blood and iron, a home for being.

But I'd arrived at a place that precision could not reach. Now there were just the tides and whims of my body. And longing, bloodred and immeasurable.

Congratulations on your pregnancy! This letter is in reference to your August 2012 IVF cycle, which I'd like to review for our records and yours.

As you know, you were on 2 ampules of Menopur per day, with the doses increasing and then decreasing due to the response. The hCG was administered on day 15 with the estradiol level at 2690. At retrieval, 14 eggs were obtained, of which 13 fertilized normally. The best two 8-cell embryos were transferred into the uterine cavity on day 3. The pregnancy test was positive on 8/23/12. Levels rose appropriately, and a singleton pregnancy resulted. Of the remaining embryos, 3 became very nice blastocysts and are also frozen for you.

We wish you the very best of luck during the pregnancy.

For days, I was possessed by rabid happiness. I floated through the rooms of our apartment in a daze, able to think of nothing but what bloomed in my core. But eventually, I sat down and did an internet search of "blastocysts." I learned that embryos reach this stage at about five days, and that those hardy enough to survive this long have a good chance of surviving longer.

When we began IVF, there'd been paperwork addressing the possibility of surplus embryos: The hospital would freeze and store these for up to three years, at which point we could, if we wished, transfer them to a private cryogenic facility. I remember how absurdly hopeful this document seemed, with its stipulations about the handling of genetic material that didn't yet—and might not ever—exist. It was strangely speculative and daunting paperwork, which is likely why I found it years later in a folder of IVF records, partially filled out and unreturned.

This was, for a long time, the start and end of my thinking about embryos. I never stopped to wonder in what sort of vessel our embryos' cells had cleaved and multiplied, or under whose watchful eye. I never thought to ask how our embryos became frozen, or how they'd become unfrozen should we need them. These details were beside the point, because these embryos were beside the point. The point was a baby, and now—belly slowly swelling, heartbeat steadily rising—we were on our delirious way to having one.

I'll never know which of the photo's two circles vanished into my bloodstream, and which lodged in me and flourished. Is it the one on the left, or the one on the right, that dissolved into nothingness? Is it the one on the right, or the one on the left, that became our son, the almond-eyed boy who burst into our lives one April afternoon, spike-haired and howling and saturated, already, with our love. The one we named Jacob, after his late paternal grandfather, and whom we've never for a moment doubted was always meant to be.

To spend your days with an infant is to live, fully and relentlessly, in the present. There's always a feeding to be done, a diaper to be changed, a bath to be given, clothes to be washed. There's the baby to be rocked in your arms until he falls asleep, and the baby to be soothed when he startles himself awake. There's the heft of his thigh against your thigh, the wet of his saliva against your shoulder, the slice of his cries in your ears, the kiss of his breath on your neck. Your mind wanders and then it is halted—the baby has giggled, tumbled over, placed a nickel in his mouth. You never do get around to calling your aunt, or making plans for a week from Tuesday, or thinking about the frozen crystals of your DNA, suspended in a tank of liquid nitrogen in the Longwood Medical Area, two miles from your house but as far away as a dream.

A baby insists on the here and now, while frozen embryos lie in wait, straddling what has been, and what might be. They keep their distance until they're summoned.

When Jacob turned one, we started getting a babysitter again. I'd put on lip gloss and Paul would shave, and we'd flee, floored by our freedom and rediscovered fondness for each other.

In the flicker of restaurant candlelight, we discussed one spring night whether to have another child. We named the cons: compounding our expenses, spreading ourselves thin, reliving the grueling first months of parenthood. We named the pros: providing our children another sibling, opening ourselves to the unexpected, leaning into a messy sort of fullness. And then I named something that was neither pro nor con, but an unavoidable third factor: our three embryos, hovering at the far edge of our life like a question that's been asked but not yet answered. A question we had no choice but to answer—and quick, for nothing threatens fertility like the ticking of the clock.

These embryos, I was beginning to understand, didn't mean the same thing to Paul as they were coming to mean to me. To him, they were an option. To me, they were a summoning, a moral quandary, a referendum on my goodness.

"But what is your *heart* telling you?" I said. "You must lean one way or the other." I longed to bring fate into this decision, or a sense of emotional inevitability. I longed for my husband to end this limbo with a flash of poetic insight.

What he said was: "We'd need to prepare ourselves to be set back a few years. We're just starting to get our lives back."

I bristled. "Is that a good reason not to have one?"

"Our life feels pretty complete to me as it is. I'm just not sure something's missing."

"I keep thinking about our embryos," I said.

"Are they a good reason to have one?"

"It sounds like you don't want one."

He frowned. "That's not what I said."

We sat at the bar of the burger place around the corner. It was summer now. Bill Withers poured from the speakers and milky evening light filtered in through the window.

"What do you think—should we have another baby?" I said.

"Is that what you want?"

"Not if it's not what you want."

Paul looked out the window, then back at me. "I want what you want," he finally said. "I want you to know I can get behind whatever you want." What I heard in these words wasn't resignation but humility—the recognition that what I'd undertaken to create our family went far beyond what he had undertaken, or even could have undertaken had he wanted to.

The door to the restaurant was open, and I could feel the July night air on my arms. My husband looked young and vital. Down the street, around the corner, on the second floor of the narrow gabled house we call our home, Jacob would be sleeping in his crib, his cheek pressed against his sheet with its pattern of forest animals, his chest rising and falling under his pajamas. Two miles away—but *where*, exactly? in an underground storage room? in some sort of medical fridge? I was realizing just how utterly I'd failed in my attention—were the multi-celled blooms we'd left behind in his wake.

How many cells was Jacob now, I wondered?

The room had grown busier, louder. My cheeks were warm, and music spilled over my skin. I knew, in this moment, what we'd be doing with those embryos. Perhaps I had always known. What other conscionable answer could there be?

A blastocyst, I've since learned, is the size of a pen tip. It contains around three hundred cells, no longer arrayed haphazardly but organized in layers. From the outer layer arises a baby's skin, brain, nerves, eyes, and inner ears. From the middle layer emerges their bones, muscles, and heart. From the innermost layer come their lungs, stomach, and bladder. In a natural pregnancy, an embryo reaches this stage at four weeks. One week later is when the heart starts beating—when the hearts of our own blastocysts, unchecked, would have started beating. The pen tip moves. Up goes the line, and then down. Up and down and up and down and up and down.

An embryo becomes frozen through a process called vitrification, from the Latin word for glass, *vitrum*. A cryoprotectant is added, drawing out water to prevent ice crystals. The embryo is plunged in liquid nitrogen, its temperature dropping within seconds from 98.6 to -300 degrees Fahrenheit. Biological time has been stopped. The cannister is sealed. Inside, the embryo lies still and glassine, a porthole in the dark.

Months pass, or years, or decades. The longest an embryo has been frozen before becoming a baby is twenty-eight years. In 2020, a Tennessee wife and husband implanted this "adopted" embryo, which had been frozen since 1992. When the wife gave birth, she was twenty-nine years old, which means she was both three decades older and roughly the same age as her daughter. Scientists believe frozen embryos could last as long as a century or two, upending our notion of lineage. Perhaps a woman will one day give birth to her great-great-grandfather's frozen sibling, or become mother to her time-stopped great-great-aunt.

The clinic instructed me to come in three days after my period for an ultrasound of my uterus. When our embryos were thawed, the vitrification process would be reversed, like a film on rewind. The cryoprotectant would be diluted and drawn out. The embryos would be warmed in air, and then in water, rising to room temperature, and then to body temperature—the temperature of my readied womb.

Now that it was coming, I waited for this moment as one waits for a long-lost relative to appear at the airport gate, or to throw her arms around a beloved friend, estranged for all these years.

There's a particular folklore in the fertility world, passed along in internet forums. A couple has tried forever to have a baby. They've tried oral medications, artificial insemination, and rounds of IVF. They've tried acupressure, acupuncture, diets of raw foods only, and diets of warm foods only. Eventually, they decide enough is enough. The trying is too painful—they can hardly remember joy. They give up and start smoking pot and making love again. And then, the unthinkable happens: Just when they're least expecting it, they conceive.

Probably I shouldn't have been surprised when the wait for my period and the ultrasound went on and on, and I found myself, two weeks late, at the CVS register with a pregnancy test kit in my hand.

At home, I uncapped the stick. I was certain there'd be only one line. And yet, to wait the three instructed minutes was to dwell, however briefly, in possibility. The drenched stick lay on the sink. I hovered a few feet away, going through life's motions, folding towels and answering a text. I edged closer, permitted my eyes to shift. One solid red line. And next to it, maybe something else, a watermark, or the sharp edge of a shadow. It was off-white, and then it was blush. Blood rose from my knees to my groin to my neck as it turned from magenta to fuchsia to a confident, deep, and wholly indisputable red.

My first thought was that something was wrong with the test. It was as if my neural pathways, so well-rutted for disappointment, fumbled to properly channel this information. I understood that getting pregnant—naturally, spontaneously—happens to women all the time, *has* happened to women for all time. But the fact that my own body could do this seemed as outlandish as discovering that my voice could break the sound barrier, or that my fingers could spin gold.

Oh my god, oh my god, I whispered. I stumbled around our bedroom, the stick in my fist, the rug like clouds under my feet. I crumpled to my knees and pounded the cloudy rug with my palms. I was like something caged released into the wild, returned, at last, to air and sunshine, to tides and seasons, to nature taking its blissfully thoughtless course.

There would be no need now for that preliminary ultrasound. No need for hormone injections to prepare my uterus. And no need, of course, to release our embryos to the timeline of the living. But I didn't think about any of this—not yet. Joy frees you from many things, at least temporarily: the burden of choice, the pain of loss, the press of conscience against your temples, constant as a headache.

• • •

One morning when he was almost two, Jacob discovered my snow boots and pulled them on. I followed him as he clomped and belly-laughed around our kitchen, egging him on and taking photos, my own belly, at six months pregnant, full and round as a globe.

My phone buzzed, and I saw that I'd missed a call. There was a voicemail from Dr. Carter. How strange to hear her voice—like a dispatch from my barren past—while I stood pregnant in a kitchen strewn with cereal and toys. She was calling to remind us that in three months, our embryos would need to be transferred to an outside center; otherwise, we could discuss options for disposal. Strange, but they didn't seem to have our authorization form on file. No problem, they'd drop one in the mail.

Later, I told Paul about the message. "I guess we'll need to transfer our embryos," I said.

He looked at me gently, bemusedly. "You know we're about to have a baby, right?"

"Yes," I said.

"Do you have some hope," he asked carefully, "of having more babies?"

"Definitely not."

"How much does it cost to store embryos?" he asked.

I'd prepared myself for this with a web search. "Seven hundred for the transfer and storage for one year, and then five hundred every year after that."

Again the bemused look, now mixed with incredulity. "So, you want us to pay thousands of dollars to hold onto embryos for a baby we'll never have?"

There was no reasonable way to answer this question, a question designed, of course, to expose unreason. But time was on my side. Three months was also when our baby was due. Even my husband, whose clear-thinking pragmatism has saved me over and over, saw that to discard our embryos now would be a wild act of hubris, with our child still inside me and not yet solid in our hands.

When our baby is truly here, I thought, when I am cradling its full weight in my arms, *then* I will be ready for closure.

Decide about embryos, I wrote in my planner. When the stapled pack of forms arrived, I placed it atop the file tray on my desk.

April came, and May, and then June. Our baby arrived, a girl, whole and perfect. I spent hours in the little park down the street, nursing her on a bench while Jacob and Leigh dangled from the swings on their bellies, pretending to fly. The baby kicked her feet in the air and batted idly at my shoulder, then slept against my chest like a slug. July passed. August came and went. It was time to pump and the burp cloths needed washing and the kids were hungry again.

Decide about embryos, I wrote afresh on my to-do list. At some point, I stopped writing it, because the writing only reminded me of my new and uncharacteristic negligence. I assumed, with both dread and hope, that the clinic would call, putting an end to this limbo.

Any day, I thought, the clinic will call.

But they never called.

A year went by, and still, they never called.

. . .

For a while, I thought of our embryos a little like insurance. *God forbid anything should happen to our children.* Should the unimaginable happen, there would be horror, despair, a descent into the darkest hopelessness. But there would not be nothing, for there would be our three embryos, waiting like life rafts to haul us up from the depths.

We are too far into our forties now, and too frayed, and too far beyond the having of babies to believe anything could lead us back to the baby stage. Our embryos have outlived this particular purpose, but the mind has a way of creating its own purposes. A new fear has risen up, replacing the old one. I'm superstitious about discarding our embryos. I worry—I'm afraid to say this— that something terrible will befall my children the moment we do. *Step on a crack, break your mother's back.* I cling to our embryos like amulets, like rabbits' feet, fearing what will happen if I let them go.

This is all to say that science can solve many things. But it cannot solve all the things. And sometimes, the problems it can't solve are the ones it has made.

What do parents like us owe our frozen embryos, those glimmers of being that wouldn't be here were it not for our yearnings, and our stunning lack of foresight? How are we to orient ourselves to them, we who donate to Planned Parenthood, who flew into fury watching a parade of white male governors sign portentous "heartbeat" bills banning abortion at a stage when many women don't even know they're pregnant? What does it mean to curse at Georgia governor Brian Kemp on your TV, with his well-fed jowls and American flag lapel pin and blather about protecting the innocent because "all life matters," while across the room sits a packet of embryo disposal consent forms, yellowing at the edges? How can I believe both these statements to be true: An early-stage embryo is not a human life. To destroy my early-stage embryos would mean ending three nascent lives.

Another year went by, and still the clinic never called. I clung to my assumption that no respectable IVF center would destroy our genetic material without informing us, because to believe otherwise would mean acknowledging I'd ceded all responsibility for our potential offspring to strangers who had no attachment to them whatsoever. Which was, of course, exactly what I'd done.

I did try to sort this out, once, about eighteen months ago, when I sat down at my desk and emailed our clinic for an update. It wasn't clarity or resolve, exactly, that prompted this, but rather a sort of low-grade embarrassment in front of myself. *What kind of a full-grown adult lets a thing like this go?* The clinic replied that our embryos were indeed still in storage, and that I must fill out a form indicating what should happen to them next. This form was—here we went again—attached. Please print, sign, and send. I told myself that I would sit down with my husband that very evening, and that we would finally do the respectable, adult thing.

Paul and I set out dinner, cleaned up, and shepherded our children to bed. We did not sit down to do the adult thing—not that night or the next. After a while, I could hardly remember what it was I intended to authorize: the preservation of our embryos, or their cessation? And so the packet remained on my desk, along with the kids' latest progress reports, the assembly instructions for our new credenza.

. . .

Time hasn't made it easier to let go. If anything, it has made it harder, because time has given the embryos a history, and history has a way of imbuing the objects of our world with weight and meaning.

When our embryos rose into existence, I was thirty-five. My forehead was smoother, my worry lines fainter. Obama was president, and I wore my hair short, and we lived in downtown Boston in a two-room rental by a park that held sundown concerts. My grandmother, who taught me how to chop onions, to oil paint, and to love without restraint, was still alive. Frozen embryos don't age. And yet, time passes, and still they're here, carrying along the past in their cells. So how can they be said not to exist in time?

Deeper still, embedded in their DNA, is time that stretches back generations—glacial layers of time, one atop the next. There are stories in these frozen layers, tales of wild endurance and last-minute escapes. I'm here because my father is here. My father is here because one day, when my grandmother was an infant in Ukraine, her parents brought her by horse and buggy to visit friends in the neighboring town. While they were gone, a pogrom raged through their village, annihilating its Jewish inhabitants. My great-grandparents returned to find their home ravaged, their entire family massacred inside it.

My husband is here because his mother is here. His mother is here because her parents saw the writing on the wall and left Berlin in 1938, before it was too late.

Of the millions of sperm that made their way from my husband into a petri dish, thirteen found their way to my waiting eggs. Of those fertilized eggs, some endured for one day, or for two, and some endured for another, and then another, until in the end, three embryos—and one boy—were left standing.

Everyone's story, in the end, is a story of survival.

I often wish I could see our embryos as clumps of cells, disposable as biopsied tissue. Instead, when I think of them, I think of my great-grandparents slipping away in the dark of night, into Poland and Hungary, past border guards they bribed with the jewels they'd stashed away so well. I think of my infant grandmother on a boat from England to Cuba, and then on to America, where she settled with her parents in a Lower East Side tenement, becoming a girl, and then a woman. When I think of our embryos, I think of the urgency in my grandmother's arms as she hugged me close, as if fulfilling a primal call to protect her own.

Every year that he grows, our son Jacob reveals himself to us more completely. He looks just like his father, who looks just like his father, dark-lashed and apple-cheeked. When he was born, his left earlobe stuck up, like a folded corner of a page, from being pressed against the wall of my womb. For weeks, as instructed, we taped it down with a sliver of surgical tape, but even now I can see how one ear cups forward ever so slightly, so that he looks like an attentive puppy.

Our son's arms are wiry, but his toes are stubby. His feet are callused from running barefoot through the woods, across pavement, up and down the stairs, and out onto the porch. Everywhere he heads, he sprints, as if the ground were crumbling beneath him.

Jacob loves pickles, raw parsley, and seafood of any sort. He's always running to tell me jokes I can hardly understand. When he's nearing the punchline, his voice grows louder and his words come out quicker and quicker. He wants so badly for me to laugh with him. And I do. Not because of the jokes, but because of his joy. His joy pries me open to laughter.

I share all this not to show that my son is so wonderful, but to show that he is *particular*. Which makes it hard not to see our embryos as particular. Maybe you are a three-layered cellular mass. Or maybe you are a boy with a Hebrew name, a puppy-dog ear, three bedroom windows looking out onto the neighbors' cherry tree.

"What should I do with my frozen embryos?" I recently inquired of a search bar. What was I hoping to find? I already knew our options, each more unsettling than the next, each waiting, arms crossed, to expose my moral failings. We could discard our embryos, closing the door on their potentiality forever. We could donate them to a couple trying to conceive—a beautifully selfless gesture as possible for me as shipping my living children away to be raised by strangers. Or we could donate our embryos to research, a path that appealed for its altruism, but left me uneasy. Whose research? And for what purpose?

If the internet has taught me anything, it's that my struggle isn't unique. There are an estimated one million frozen embryos in the United States. Up to a third of these, researchers believe, are still here because their creators cannot decide what to do with them. They exist, like our embryos, in double limbo, suspended between non-life and life, and then suspended again in the slush of indecision. The dilemma is so common that there's an official term for it: "embryo disposition."

This ambivalence has led to another problem raising alarm among bioethicists, which when I first read its name, made my skin tense with recognition: the problem of "abandoned embryos." When the "owner" of frozen embryos has failed to pay storage fees, when she has neglected to respond to written correspondence—when she has left the required paperwork moldering on her desk for half a decade—then her embryos can be considered "abandoned." One paper in *Nature Biotechnology* asserts there are at least 90,000 abandoned embryos in the United States. Other studies suggest there could be far more. I am but one example of this most modern deadbeat parent, all of us shirking responsibility for our creations while banking on an assumption that turns out to be right: Fertility clinics, I learned, are extremely unlikely to get rid of abandoned embryos for fear of being charged with wrongful death or ending up at the center of a media storm. A partner at the International Fertility Law Group has said he doesn't know of a single clinic willing to dispose of them.

There's comfort in discovering that the problem you've been wrestling with is a collective problem, when all along you've borne it as a private struggle. I understood for the first time that the problem of my embryos—the problem of *all* surplus embryos—didn't arise by happenstance. It had a cause. And while my husband and I were certainly part of this cause, with our myopic determination, by any means necessary, to produce a baby, so, too, was a fertility industry that sustains this myopia. For this industry is as much a part of our culture as any, and as addicted to the nearsighted belief that more is better. And so it breeds, quite literally, an excess of human possibility. It says, *Here, we have made for you these pulsing diamonds—more than you will ever want or need! It is completely up to you what you will do with them.*

· · ·

"Hope is the thing with feathers— / That perches on the soul— / And sings the tune without the words— / And never stops—at all—" wrote Emily Dickinson. These lines, nestled in my brain since high school, have been returning to me lately—in bed, in the shower—offering a glimpse of resolution, a nudge toward an answer.

What keeps us parents going—sustaining heartbreak after heartbreak, wearing ourselves down daily—if not hope, that thing perched inside us, crooning that the lives we're nurturing will be good lives, lived by good people, who will go off to do good things? Love is itself a form of hope. I've started to understand that what seizes in my chest when I imagine closing the door on our embryos is the pain of letting go of potential—no matter how unsuited my circumstances now are to this potential. As a mother, I've been trained to worship in the temple of what *could* be. And an embryo is a powerful, nuclear hope, dense and enormous.

But an experienced mother knows that devotion is our calling through all seasons—when our children are budding and flourishing, yes, but also when they are bumping up against their limitations. We watch them learn who they are, but also who they'll never be, as thousands of potentialities fall from them day after day, like so many sloughed-off cells. We who create life love beginnings, but we must also learn to love denouements, conclusions, and the daily falling action that permeates motherhood. We must come to accept that every beginning contains a kernel of loss.

Gwendolyn Brooks's "the mother" begins: "Abortions will not let you forget. / You remember the children you got that you did not get." I reread this poem recently after a space of many years. Twenty-four hours earlier, the Supreme Court had overturned *Roe v. Wade*, reversing fifty years of reproductive freedom in a single stroke and toppling me into a despair I saw no way out of. I'd been submerged for hours in a slurry of news articles and opinion pieces, each more terrifying and dire than the next. I needed something—anything—that might give my grief form and direction.

In my memory, "the mother" was a poem about abortion and the sorrow its speaker experiences in the aftermath of her own. But reading it again, years after teaching Brooks's poetry to high school seniors, I saw that it was a meditation not only on loss, but on maternal love in its fullest form. The speaker's unborn children are still, in their absence, her children, and she conjures them with the tender attention of a mother, maternal devotion pervading even this most seemingly un-maternal act. Addressing her never-born offspring, Brooks's mother character offers this claim of responsibility: "Sweets, if I sinned, if I seized / Your luck / And your lives from your unfinished reach, / . . . If I poisoned the beginnings of your breaths / Believe that even in my deliberateness I was not deliberate."

Brooks's poem subverts all assumptions about what it means to care for children. It insists that mothering can mean many things, and that each woman alone knows, at a given time, what it must mean for her. I've been waiting all these years for the magic appearance of a path that feels fully right. But there isn't one. No one terminates a pregnancy because it's easy; no one destroys her embryos because it's easy. There's no freedom or closure in these decisions—only a coming to terms.

"Believe me, I loved you all," the mother-speaker declares at the end of Brooks's poem. "Believe me, I knew you, though faintly, and I loved, I loved you / All."

. . .

The term "abandoned embryo" reminded me that inaction is its own action, and it, too, can have disastrous consequences. The potential consequences of abandoning an embryo aren't ones I like thinking about. Leaving it for one's children to have to grapple with, letting it fall into ill-intentioned hands—there's nowhere my imagination won't go.

So many of our human inventions replicate the patterns of nature. Japan's Shinkansen bullet train was inspired by the beak of the kingfisher, Velcro by the tiny hooks of bur fruits. Assisted reproduction is no different. A needle pierces a woman's skin, and her body is awakened. She opens herself to the ultrasound probe, slick with lubricant, the catheter spilling forth its seed. In vitro fertilization takes the sweating, breathing, messy cycle of procreation and recreates it in titrated, sterilized form. We accept this version not only because it's our only option, but because even in its unnaturalness, it approximates the natural, so that beneath its cold sterility, it feels familiar.

But what's the natural equivalent of discarding one's embryos? Here's where I have stumbled, again and again.

It's possible that when you invite technology into the most intimate recesses of your life, you forfeit your right to wax poetic about the natural order of things. But I'm beginning to wonder, too, what "the natural order of things" really means. "Our technology both extends and endangers us," writes author Eula Biss in her book *On Immunity*. "Good or bad, it is part of us, and this is no more unnatural than it is natural."

I don't know exactly what day our blastocysts were destroyed. When I picture them, they're still suspended in darkness, descending on me dimly, as if through a moonlit sky. I see three circles, small and sparkling. They float down like snowflakes, their delicate sticking crystals light as air. They spin and glisten in the night, falling and falling, and then they touch down on earth, where they soften, melt, and dissolve away. They dissolve like snowflakes on a lake, or like snowflakes on the surface of the ocean.

But no, this isn't right. They dissolve like the embryos they are, subsiding to water in a plastic dish, swirling away—considered, known, loved—into the bloodstream of the world.

Thinkers Who Mother

The most profound compliment I've received in my years as a mother came from a bearded hipster in a plaid shirt working the register at my local bookstore. This was at the end of a Saturday morning spent carting Nora along with me on errands. We'd made it through the pharmacy, the dry cleaner, and the grocery store, finally arriving there, where I could reward her patience with the purchase of a picture book. One grew into two, and then, *alright*, *three*—because books are books, and it's hard for me to deny them to anyone.

A purple paperclip holder in the shape of cat is not a book. But the moment Nora spotted this item by the register, she had to have it. "Mama, look!" she said, her voice both grave and exuberant. As a seasoned mother, I knew this tone well. I piled our books on the counter, glancing down just long enough to make my decision: "We're just getting books today, Lovie." I knew—because I know four-year-olds—that this conversation wasn't over. She tried insistence. *But Mommy*. She tried logic. *I really, really need it*. She tried promises. *I'll never ask for anything again*. With each attempt, I could see her body growing more rigid, her fists curling tighter. Meanwhile, the guy behind the counter had finished ringing up our purchases. Someone was waiting behind me. I grew hot under my jacket. I needed to do something quickly.

If this were six years earlier and my oldest child, I would've caved in desperation. If it were three years earlier and my middle child, I would've resolutely reminded him that money doesn't grow on trees while he collapsed in a weeping heap on the bookstore floor. Today, I drew upon all my years of surprise triumphs and near misses and outright disasters to try a third approach. "You love that cat! I can see why. It's really cute."

Nora's shoulders lowered slightly. I had her ear—but where was this going? "Do you want to put it on your Hanukkah wish list?" I said. She didn't actually have such a list—I'd invented it that very moment.

"But you won't *remember* it," she said. "You won't remember what it *is*!" She was panicked, tense. It has taken me years to understand that the desire of a young child—no matter how trivial its object may seem—is as real and acute as any grown-up desire. I couldn't lessen my daughter's longing. But I just might, I hoped, be able to lessen her worry.

I took out my phone. "I have an idea. Let's take a photo, so you can know for sure I'll remember it." This was a gamble. The line behind us was growing. But a tantrum would be worse for all of us. Nora looked up at me. She loves to see how my phone camera works, how the full moon circle makes the picture stick to the screen and then live in my phone forever. I kneeled down, and she came to me. Together, we held up the phone, centering it on the cat's whiskered face. She lifted her fingertip to the circle. The phone clicked, and she nodded triumphantly.

Behind the counter, the man in the plaid shirt slipped our books into a shopping bag and then uttered the sentence that would fill me with a deeper sense of accomplishment than any of my life's milestones, or any of my academic achievements or career successes. "I have to tell you," he said, "how beautiful it was watching you handle that."

By the time I'd processed these words, my nose was tingling and my eyes were stinging, and it felt like something had unlatched inside my chest. I felt such gratitude for this stranger, this young man in plaid, who'd acknowledged something in me that hadn't been acknowledged before, that I'd never quite acknowledged myself. I could not have said in that moment what, exactly, this thing was, and why its recognition had touched me so.

"I wish I could explain how much that means to me," I told him.

I am still trying.

It's commonly said that being a mother "is the hardest job there is." On the surface, this would seem the ultimate compliment. But I've become suspicious of this type of praise, which—in a country that denies women paid maternal leave, all but ignores postpartum health, and offers no systematized childcare solutions—strikes me as inauthentic. I think of an archetypal 1950s father walking in after work while his wife pulls a roast from the oven and herds the children toward the table: "I don't know how you do it, Dear," he might say between forkfuls. "The hardest job there is!"

Platitudes like this link motherhood with martyrdom and sacrifice—characteristics of the idealized motherhood Adrienne Rich describes in her book *Of Woman Born*. By framing motherhood as a "sacred calling"—the apex of female becoming—our culture may put mothers on a pedestal, but in ways that erase our complexity and ignore our wholeness. There's no recognition, in this sentimentalized version of motherhood, of the complicated, nuanced, mental work raising humans actually demands. Nor is there acknowledgment that mothers, too, are people on their own path of creation, learning and evolving daily.

"Most mothers are instinctive philosophers," wrote Harriet Beecher Stowe, a notion that PhD philosopher Sara Ruddick picks up in her essay "Maternal Thinking." Because it's so deeply associated with feeling, we "often remain ignorant of the perspective, the *thought* that has developed from mothering," she writes. Ruddick shows how a mother—as she nourishes and morally shapes a human life—engages in the discipline of maternal thinking, as serious and rigorous as any "religious, scientific, historical" or "mathematical" discipline. It's no coincidence that these examples come from realms traditionally dominated by men, highlighting an age-old binary that privileges intellect over emotion, and logic over intuition. Ruddick rejects this division, showing how intellect *and* feeling merge to fuel the work of mothering.

It might seem obvious to point out that mothering involves thinking. After all, mothers are humans—*of course* they think. But Western history is riddled with examples of attempts to pit intellect against maternity, brain against uterus. After the 1856 publication of *Madame Bovary,* fear spread of a phenomenon called "Bovarysme": Experts warned that reading was becoming a dangerous epidemic among women, severing them from their natural female role. Because of their "lower brain weight," doctors posited, women risked overstimulating their minds with books, jeopardizing their reproductive organs and fertility. In 1890, when suffering from what would likely now be diagnosed as postpartum depression, "The Yellow Wallpaper" author Charlotte Perkins Gilman received a similar warning from her doctor: "Have but two hours intellectual life a day. And never touch pen, brush or pencil as long as you live."

It would be easy to laugh off this attitude as a Victorian relic if shades of it didn't persist. To be sure, women today are far more appreciated for their intellectual capacities—in academia, in the workplace, and in public life. But when a woman walks out into the world as a mother, these capacities tend to be obscured by her overarching mother-ness—and the artistry and intellectual rigor *of* mothering are hardly recognized at all. The most common modern showcase for maternal thought might be the "mommy blog," a term that, in its cuteness, captures our culture's infantilization of mothers, and its refusal to take our thoughts seriously. Advice books like *The Happiest Toddler on the Block* or *Moms on Call*—to name a couple on my bookshelf—do, in their way, treat mothering as a craft that can be practiced and refined, and yet they take as their basic premise mothers' helplessness to tackle, uninstructed, the practical and moral questions of raising a child. Tellingly, to this day, the most revered gurus of this genre—Harvey Karp, T. Berry Brazelton, Benjamin Spock, William Sears—are mostly men.

In the early 2000s, *Salon* housed a column called "Mothers Who Think." Possibly, this title was meant to be a little cheeky. But in distinguishing thinking as something unusual enough to call out, it confirmed the *unthinking* mother as the norm. The fact that the women writing for this section were largely privileged, educated, and white made this title even more troubling, suggesting that while some mothers—elite mothers—engage regularly in complex thinking, the common horde of moms out there do not.

I was a recent college graduate when this column appeared— single, childless, and thrilled to have landed a job as an editorial assistant at a New York City publishing house. Eating lunch at my desk, I'd sometimes scroll through *Salon*, passing over "Mothers Who Think" as irrelevant to me. At the time, this title didn't strike me as troublesome, which reveals to me just how steeped I was in our culture's ideas of maternity. As an eager, career-oriented, young adult woman whose greatest passions were books and writing, I had no trouble at all conceiving of myself as a thinker. I'd been encouraged my whole life—by my family, at my rigorous all-girls high school, in college—to be a thinker. But at no time had I been prepared to be a mother-thinker, or to see motherhood as a cerebral undertaking.

I *had* been prepared to be a mother, in all the ways girls are groomed to become mothers. But from my twenty-two-year-old vantage point, the mother in me had little to do with the thinker in me—for as far as I was concerned, mothers operated outside the world of ideas and power, in a sealed, pastel kingdom of mobiles and lullabies. I might one day become a mother, but for now, the mother in me waited deep in my cells, a tangle of instinct and urge that would eventually kick in—presumably around age thirty—replacing the thinking, striving me with something gentler. This mother was a separate person from my current self, and like two characters played by the same actor, we couldn't be on stage simultaneously.

If this future wrecking ball to my intellectual life concerned me at the time, it was only in a distant way. And in any case, once that baby emerged and floated into my arms, surely I wouldn't mind so much. Surely, my subsumption into the realm of feeling would be a delicious and powder-sweet surrender.

The only cultural touchpoint I can think of that connects mothering and thought is a demeaning one, and that's the term "mommy brain," used to describe the forgetfulness women with young babies sometimes experience. The indignity of this term has no bottom. A woman who has just brought forth new life—who perseveres through sleeplessness and extraordinary physical and psychic changes in order to study, understand, and nurture this new life—has as her command center something far more fearsome than a "mommy brain."

Over time, I've stumbled upon far truer representations of the "mommy brain," which I turn to more and more. I am thankful every day for the poems of Rita Dove and Sharon Olds, for the essays of Jacqueline Rose and Alice Walker, and for the fiction of Louise Erdrich and Carol Shields. How, I now wonder, did I make it through most of my adult life without reading Alice Munro, whose stories became a ballast for me in the midstream of motherhood?

Munro doesn't just depict mothers thinking: She imbues this thinking with all the import and tension of any classic heroic journey. Take her story "My Mother's Dream." Told from the perspective of her now-grown baby daughter, this story focuses on Jill, a conservatory violinist and World War II–era bride widowed during pregnancy. Taken in by her sisters-in-law, she spends the hours before labor ravenous and insatiable, an ungoverned creature who eats her way through the day, fueled by an "irritability amounting almost to panic that makes her stuff into her mouth what she can hardly taste any longer." This imagery is a far cry from our culture's archetypal mother-to-be—quietly expectant as she spends her final childless days "nesting."

Jill continues to stumble over motherhood's script. For starters, she utterly fails at breastfeeding, that consummate emblem of maternal achievement. "I screamed blue murder," the daughter-narrator tells us. "The big stiff breast might just have been a snouted beast rummaging in my face." The newborn daughter rejects her mother's milk in favor of formula, and her mother's arms in favor of the arms of Iona, Jill's nervous and obliging sister-in-law.

We all know what Jill is supposed to feel in this moment. Guilt, failure, and the piercing self-incrimination so many flesh-and-blood mothers I know have suffered when they, too, have struggled to establish breastfeeding, a process far more complicated and grueling than any Renaissance painting would have us believe. Instead, Jill welcomes her baby's preference for Iona, which frees her up to turn her attention back to the violin. But in her first postpartum attempt to play, everything comes out wrong. Her daughter wakes crying, further thwarting her. The daughter-narrator reflects:

> How can I describe what music is to Jill? Forget about landscapes and visions and dialogues. It is more of a problem... that she has taken on as her responsibility in life. Suppose then that the tools that serve her for working on this problem are taken away. The problem is still there in its grandeur... but it is removed from her. For her, just the back step and the glaring wall and my crying. My crying is a knife to cut out of her life all that isn't useful. To me.

Jill is conquered by a version of motherhood in which feeling and intellect cannot coexist, and the overthrow is crushing.

I have lived this version of motherhood, having endured, in my early years as a mother, a flattening of my creative self equally violent and complete. It's music that eludes Jill; for me, it was writing, the one pursuit that had ever anchored me, as inseparable from who I was as my body or name. From the time I could write,

I wrote, filling notebooks with stories as a child, and scrawling poems on loose-leaf paper as a teenager. In my twenties, I fell in love with nonfiction, the way words could be a magnifying glass for truth. And always I kept journals. Countless journals.

For nearly thirty years, I wrote. And then I had a baby, and I no longer wrote.

I don't mean that I wrote less frequently, or less prolifically. I stopped abruptly and altogether, as if a vein had been cauterized. When friends asked what I was working on, I'd tell them the same lie I'd told myself, that it was "so hard to find the time with the baby!" Like most good lies, there was a grain of truth in this. Being our daughter's primary caregiver did shrink the time I had to use creatively. But this wasn't the full story. What stood between me and writing wasn't mothering: It was striving to mother perfectly—to become, fully and completely, that golden idol worthy of adulation.

I extended my leave from my English teaching job and reorganized my life with my daughter at its center. No store-bought baby food for my girl; instead, I stood for hours in my kitchen, fussing over pots of stewing vegetables, then ladling them into labeled freezer trays. No fitness center daycare for my baby; instead, I heaved her down city blocks during group stroller walks, straining for conversation with the band of mothers I'd fallen in with. I attended a playgroup or baby enrichment class every day of the week—and for a period of time on Thursdays, two playgroups in one day. I poked at Play-Doh in art class, shook tiny maracas in music class, and read picture books aloud at the library until my throat felt angry and tight.

I became depressed. On the phone with an old friend, I cried out, "*All* my creativity is going into my child." Here, finally, was something closer to the truth. But it wasn't exactly creativity I was channeling into my daughter. Rather, it was a sort of frantic, white-knuckled enactment of the mother I believed I must be, an enactment that required nearly all my energy and will. To admit my writerly self into my motherhood was to jeopardize the entire fragile persona I'd created.

The mother ideal, I've come to believe, is uniquely insidious, because what we feel to be at stake is so precious to us, and so at the mercy of our choices. For me, falling short of this ideal meant failing not just myself but the vulnerable human whose flourishing, I'd been led to believe, was exquisitely calibrated to my every move. Every part of my daughter's being—her petal-curled fingers, her warm bread scent, her breath against my neck—told me I had no choice.

I love "My Mother's Dream" because it reveals a pathway out of this black-and-white thinking. When Iona leaves town for a night, Jill experiences a harrowing twenty-four hours. Her baby rages nonstop, inconsolable. In the middle of this, Jill takes out her violin and attempts again to play. Any temptation to see this as neglect of maternal duty is complicated by that fact that the person most entitled to a claim of victimhood—the now-grown baby—does not. "In a way, she does me an honor," the narrator says. "No more counterfeit soothing, no more pretend lullabies or concern for tummy-ache, no petsy-wetsy whatsamatter. Instead, she will play Mendelssohn's Violin Concerto." Jill's daughter admires her integrity. Which makes me wonder: For whom do we perform sacred motherhood, if not our children?

Is Jill abusive? Negligent? Munro challenges such tidy conclusions. Even as she suffers, she continues to plod through the devotions of mothering an infant, warming bottle after bottle and washing her baby's clothes. Hammered by a headache, Jill makes a decision that should by any standard measure of a mother's goodness tip her into the category of "bad mother," and that is her choice to sprinkle shavings of her headache medication into her baby's milk. But this isn't a standard motherhood tale. When Jill's sisters-in-law return the next morning, they discover a baby who momentarily *seems* dead, but who—defying both narrative and moral expectations—is simply sleeping extremely deeply.

If Jill were a classic "good mother," she would not, of course, have fed her baby pulverized painkillers. What she is instead is a *real* mother, and in the fullness of her reality, there's space for darkness, frailty, desperation—even grave misjudgment. What's more, it's not instinct or a yielding to "sacred" duty that ultimately sets Jill on a sustainable path as a mother, but reason and will: "Sobered and grateful, not even able to risk thinking about what she'd just escaped, she took on loving me, because the alternative to loving was disaster," the narrator tells us. Mothering, like any rigorous practice, involves error, and learning from error.

As the story draws to its close, we feel reassured that Jill has found a version of motherhood more aligned with her own particularities. And what has this truth nurtured? Our narrator, her daughter, who speaks of her own imperfect, grappling thinker-mother with the balance, humor, and insight of someone who turned out well—whose mother, in the end, must have done something right.

Real life seldom affirms the thinker-mother in this way.

Looking back on my own entry into motherhood, I can see now how the world pressed its chisel to me, slowly sculpting me into its maternal image. This shaping began in pregnancy. As my stomach rounded, the world claimed me in a way it never had before. On street corners, I was smiled upon by strangers, bathed in almost overwhelming approval. At the high school where I taught English, coworkers I hardly knew placed annointing hands on the sweater stretched over my belly. I was fulfilling my biological destiny, achieving in a way that was unambiguously good. The threads of my being that had formerly connected me to others all receded, replaced by the topic of my body and its incremental shifts, the nursery purchases completed or planned, the growing fact of my impending motherhood.

This shift went into strange acceleration when, at twenty-two weeks pregnant, I went for a routine ultrasound and was placed by my obstetrician on immediate bed rest. She explained that my cervix had "shortened," something that happens when labor is near, but my due date was months away. Shortening this early could suggest "cervical incompetence," which could lead to premature birth. I didn't need it explained to me that birth at twenty-two weeks was a potential death sentence for my baby.

My obstetrician handed me a gown. On the exam table, I lay back on the cold padding with a monitor strapped to my abdomen. I blinked up at the ceiling tiles, feeling as if my mind had been lifted and separated from my body. My mind was up there in those tiles, irrelevantly floating, and down below was my body, its vagaries and fluctuations holding me at their mercy.

That morning, I'd been the chair of an English department, in charge of a cadre of teachers and three classes of students. Now, I was a vessel charged with not cracking open. Sent home to my apartment, I saw the agenda for my next department meeting sitting absurdly on my desk; a half-written lesson plan for my poetry class hovering pointlessly on my laptop screen. Without time to panic about the fallout for me and Paul should I lose my salary, I called my head of school and told her, as if reading from a surrealist movie script, that I would not be returning tomorrow, or the next week, or the next week—and that I could not say exactly when I would.

I lay down and stayed down for days that turned into weeks and then months, rising only to use the bathroom, or to occasionally bathe, or to walk stiffly to the kitchen to eat the lunch Paul had prepared for me. Someone dropped off a DVD box set of *Lost*, and I watched all ten discs in a way that had no start or finish. I stared at my computer and scrutinized baby seats, comparing the ones that bounced to the ones that swung to the ones that bounced and swung. When I could concentrate, I read, lying on my side until my shoulder ached, and then turning onto my other side until that shoulder ached. Outside my bedroom window, the golden leaves turned brown and then disappeared, leaving behind stiff bare branches that didn't change at all until the snow came, and then they were like pale, bony arms. Dark came earlier. Mornings, I'd move from the bed to the couch, and evenings, from the couch to the bed, my mind dulled past the point of yearning.

I wish I read then, as I have now, Turkish novelist Elif Shafak's memoir *Black Milk*. Shafak's account of her pregnancy and postpartum depression is nothing like the breezy books then piled on my nightstand—like *What to Expect When You're Expecting* and *What to Expect the First Year*. Her whole adult life, Shafak has felt as if she contains a "mini-harem" within her, a "gang of females who constantly fight for nothing and bicker, looking for an opportunity to trip one another up." She attributes her success as a woman writer to the triumph of her more hard-nosed selves—"Little

Miss Practical," "Miss Highbrowed Cynic," "Milady Ambitious Chekhovian"—over the part of herself that wants children. But when Shafak unintentionally becomes pregnant, this balance collapses. Her inner mother, a frumpy tyrant named "Mama Rice Pudding," rises to the throne and rules with an iron fist, demanding that Shafak eat fatty foods for the baby, play opera for the baby, do prenatal yoga for the baby. There's "a thin line," Shafak observes, following these commands to the letter, "between motherhood and fascism." Things hardly improve after her baby is born: Shafak looks on, despairing, as her writing life morphs into a "distant and forbidden land with bulky guards protecting its boundaries."

I imagine Shafak would be unsurprised to learn, as I did from scouring the internet during my captivity, that there's no medical evidence bed rest does anything to prevent pre-term labor. (Five years later, the American College of Obstetricians and Gynecologists would release a statement advising doctors to stop recommending it.) Bed rest was—and still often is— prescribed because, quite simply, in the face of possible fetal demise, doctors need *something* to prescribe. That this something is a full-blown assault on a woman's complexity and wholeness—her absolute reduction to a biological function—is telling. Such a prescription could only exist in a world where complex and whole women are generally not the goal, and where smaller-scale attacks on mothers' humanity are commonplace.

And yet, even after bed rest had been revealed to me as little more than superstition, I surrendered myself to the beige cushions of my couch. What else could I do? This wasn't a time to probe or to challenge, for I had a baby to protect.

When, at thirty-two weeks' gestation, this baby was still in my womb, my doctor released me back into the world. I carried my daughter to term, and then beyond term, at which point I was told I might need to be induced. "Huh!" my doctor said at my forty-week appointment, in the tone of someone discovering a stray button behind a couch cushion. "This must just be your cervix's physiology!" I didn't think to say anything that would have hinted at the enormity of this error that had plundered my livelihood and identity. For at this point, my novitiate was nearing its end, and I'd been primed to enter into my self-sacrificing—and wholly sacred—calling.

If pregnancy sets in motion women's reorientation from the cerebral to the biological, early motherhood has a way of cementing it. Having read about the difficulty new mothers can have breastfeeding, I was filled with pride when my own milk exuberantly announced itself hours after I'd given birth. I looked down at my newborn daughter, who latched right on, and felt intense relief. This wasn't the relief of knowing my baby was being nourished, but rather, the full-body elation one might feel while being honored for a distinctive award. "You're a milk goddess!" one of the postpartum nurses exclaimed when checking on my progress. For the first time ever, I felt a surge of pride in my body's own involuntary functioning, as if the workings of my mammary glands were somehow proof of my virtue and worth.

Producing breastmilk, of course, has nothing to do with virtue or worth, any more than being able to conceive or carry a fetus to term—or breathe or sweat, for that matter. And yet, how accomplished I felt as I slipped right into character! I carried Leigh in one of those slings that made us look like we'd sprung from the earth. I signed us up for a Mommy and Me class to broaden my repertoire of children's songs. I took photos of her and dangled them on Facebook for people to coo over. Who knew what pathways my mind forged in those early months as a mother, what inner dialogues, what silently negotiated compromises, what dark turns and difficult revelations? I hardly acknowledged these myself—and why should I? Following the script of "good" motherhood, I felt the world's recognition wash over me, and I experienced it as personal triumph.

In a culture that denies mothers' thinking skills and rewards their compliance, is it any wonder that mothers might fail to claim the full breadth and potential of their maternal practice? Sara Ruddick explains how "out of maternal powerlessness, in response to a society whose values it does not determine," many mothers fall back on ways of being that are not wholly authentic, not wholly their own. "Inauthenticity," she explains, "gives rise to the values of obedience and being 'good'" so that "to fulfill the values of the dominant culture is taken as an achievement." A "good" mother, she notes, "may well be praised in colluding in her own subordination."

Yes! What a pleasure it was, in my early months of motherhood, to hear my mother-in-law fawn over my devotion to my colicky baby daughter, my patience, my tenderness, my sainthood. What a joy it was to hear my own mother tell me that I was "a natural," as if mothering were a knack one either has or doesn't. These were well-meaning compliments, and the happiness and fervor they affirmed weren't entirely imagined. Motherhood, for me, *has* been filled with moments of intense fulfillment and joy, but like stars in a vast night sky, it's the surrounding space that gives these their shape and sparkle.

What happens in this space is maternal thought—sometimes bright, sometimes troublingly dark, sometimes gray and hazy—but always more layered and nuanced than anything a mother is regaled for around a Mother's Day brunch table.

So how can a woman resist the sweet siren call of the mother ideal? How can she carve out a motherhood that's not a projection of others' fantasies, but an authentic expression of her values?

The museums and cathedrals and theaters of this world swarm with hallowed mothers but provide few models of thinker-mothers. I'd argue that Shafak, enacting on paper the movements of her maternal mind, stands as one example, offering a blueprint for others. The first step, her memoir suggests, is to examine with clear eyes the ways our culture pushes mothers toward conformity, so we can resist these pressures. The next step would be to bring to light the truths of motherhood, as Shafak does, by making visible the puzzles and trials and devastations concealed behind its blisses and triumphs. These will vary from woman to woman, from circumstance to circumstance, for the challenges of a white, married, heterosexual stay-at-home mother can't possibly be the same as those of a mother who works two jobs, or a divorced mother, or a Latina mother, or a lesbian mother, or a teenage mother, or any overlapping combination of these identities and more. The point is that dismantling mythical motherhood will require regular public doses of the real, whatever its form.

Shafak's imagery is also instructive. Division and fragmentation permeate her descriptions of womanhood. The selves in her "inner harem"—writer, cynic, spiritual seeker, mother—constantly bump up against one another, forming a "Choir of Discordant Voices" that can't find harmony.

This imagery brings me back again to that twenty-two-year-old I once was, who sat at her desk conceiving of womanhood and motherhood as two distinct, sequential states of being, united solely by the fact of her femaleness. I had no idea then that the qualities I'd one day bring to motherhood—contemplativeness, drive, skepticism—were the exact ones that had always been part of me. I wonder if Shafak would have felt so completely divided from her writing self had she not been primed to dissociate this part of her from her nurturing self. By the end of her memoir, her postpartum depression has dissipated, giving her space to reconcile, in a new way, the women who live inside her. These women have come to understand "that to exist freely and equally, they need one another, and that where even one voice is enslaved, none can be free." Shafak has arrived at a place, however tenuous, where mothering and thought can coexist—where, in fact, the mothering *is* the thought, for it's also at this moment that her art, her memoir, has been completed, shaped from the raw material of gestating and raising a child.

In the hours and days following the birth of my first baby, I swiftly learned that motherhood wasn't a dormant state that lay in wait in me. Were I to have relied on "maternal instinct" alone to keep my tiny daughter's brain and body nourished, her heart pumping, her body warm, and her nervous system settled, I would have failed. And as my children have turned from babies to preschoolers to elementary schoolers—and in the case of my oldest, a preteen—instinct has only become a less reliable guide. Each day, my kids' needs become more complicated, their struggles more unpredictable. And all the while, I, too, am shifting, recalibrating, gaining new wisdom and letting go of old beliefs. In my mothering, I am anything but a sacred Madonna. I am a determined shapeshifter, readjusting as I grapple my way through a role I must invent as I go.

I love my children fiercely. But being a mother requires more than love. And while it may be my heart that fuels my maternal work, the work itself, I've come to understand, is fundamentally an undertaking of the mind. For we are thinkers before we are mothers, and it is from our thinking that our mothering is born.

To identify this mind-work, it has helped me to consider how my mothering has evolved. These changes are barely detectable in the day to day but spectacularly clear in retrospect. Thinking back on my moves as a newer mother, I cringe at my rookie errors, and it's all I can do to keep from falling on my knees to beg forgiveness of my oldest, the primary victim of my inexperience. Today, when Nora heads to preschool with shorts over her pants and a wolf-ear headband, I remember with a stab of pain how I'd make Leigh, at the same age, "look presentable." When I open a box of frozen pizza instead of cooking, I no longer feel like a domestic failure but appreciate the gift of an hour of relaxed togetherness. Once upon a time, I hid from my children my sadnesses and regrets, my frustrations and confusions, equating good mothering with unimpeachable polish. Now, I remind myself that it's okay to show them my cracks—that these, in fact, help teach them what it means to be human.

In my most authentic moments as a mother, I understand fully how the work of mothering can become, in the words of Ruddick, "a rewarding, disciplined expression of conscience."

Every day I make mistakes—mistakes I'll no doubt cringe over one day. But I keep learning and experimenting, refining and expanding my practice, knowing that to conceive of mothering as a discipline is to recognize its immense importance, and to imbue it with the dignity it deserves.

This morning, when I let Nora mix grape juice into her oatmeal, I was thinking. When I helped Jacob shade in the scales of a sea-serpent, I was thinking. When I stopped myself from reminding Leigh to put her homework folder in her backpack, I was thinking.

At drop-off, at pickup, in the pharmacy line, the mothers are thinking. They are thinking in waiting rooms, on the phone with doctors, in line at the food bank, and on the way to the barber. In happiness they are thinking, and in anger, and in boredom. At home, at work, in the rumble of subway tunnels, they are thinking; and at bedtime, at naptime, at the press of a hand to their side in the middle of the night, they are thinking again.

I would like to believe my children will see a day when motherhood, like a statue turned to flesh, is returned in its wholeness to the world. It will take all of us to haul maternal thinking into the open, where it can grow and flourish, transforming from private endeavor to collective force.

On the sidewalk, a mother will wait while her son rescues a caterpillar from the path of pedestrians, and we will see her thinking. At the playground, two mothers will make a game for their children of picking up plastic water bottles, and we will see them thinking. Pediatricians will acknowledge the acuity of mothers' thinking. Mothers will be hired, promoted—elected—for the maternal agility of their thinking.

Yesterday, I wrote a note to my mother, thanking her for the steady intelligence of her parenting. Today, I will call my friend Mira, and I will map for her the genius of her mothering.

Tomorrow, maybe it will be you. Which thinker will you recognize for her mothering? Which mother will you recognize for her thinking?

Stop her. Tell her. Make her eyes burn. Across the world the chain will grow, like so many synapses firing.

Tikkun Olam Ted

In his first grade classroom at Hebrew school, Jacob and I are drawing what we plan to do to repair the world. Nora, tagging along for the morning, is also completing this assignment, and though she's slightly young for it, she gets the basic idea. She scribbles blotches of flowers on her paper while I add a woman—me?—beside a compost bin, depositing food scraps. I'm feeling pretty good about myself for being down here on the rug, in the thick of things, while most parents sit in a semicircle of chairs, watching from afar. *I am a very engaged mother*, I think. *I am modeling enthusiasm!*

It's been a trying weekend, with Paul out of town, just me and the three kids alone—a weekend of back seat feuds and bedtime brawls, cereal bowls upended and dishes piled up in the sink. I've been vexed by an irritability I don't feel entitled to, that fills me with shame each time I think of the millions of single mothers who do this day in and day out. But I've made it to Sunday morning. Sun streams through the classroom window and the air smells of cherry-scented markers, and before me stretch three hours of activities that I don't need to plan, in a space—our synagogue—that feels like a second home.

Jacob's marker scritch-scratches away. He bites the soft flesh of his lower lip and shields his work with his arm, and I keep a respectful distance, knowing how he loves to craft surprises. After a while, he snaps on his marker cap and holds up his work. I see that it's not a picture after all, but a row of words wobbling across the page. My son, who as a toddler had a speech delay, has been struggling at school to write words beyond his name, and I feel a surge of pride in this effort—a surge that lasts just long enough for me to discern what he has written. Could it be? No. But oh my god, yes. *I LUV MI PENES.*

This message clashes so profoundly with the spirit of this morning's event that I can hardly register it. We are here for an annual tradition at my children's Hebrew school, Tikkun Olam Day. The phrase *tikkun olam* means "repairing the world" and captures an idea at the heart of Judaism—that the universe is innately good but imperfect, and that our task as human beings is to help restore it to wholeness. *Tikkun olam* is often associated with social activism, but as Rabbi Zecher—who made history at our temple by becoming its first female senior rabbi three years prior— has reminded the students during today's opening assembly, our world teems with small opportunities for repair work. Conserving water is *tikkun olam*. Giving to charity is *tikkun olam*. Opening the door for someone, expressing thanks, welcoming guests into one's home—these, too, are *tikkun olam*. I've long admired Rabbi Zecher, who is extraordinarily wise and learned and also beautiful, her face warmly luminous beneath a halo of silver-white hair. And while this introductory talk was meant for the children, it moved me, as her words so often move me, to remember all the ways that I can do better.

Later in the morning, Jacob's class will prepare trays of lasagna for Rosie's Place, a local shelter for homeless women. Their teacher Morah Elena, who has crinkly eyes and a pixie haircut, has just finished reading them *Tikkun Olam Ted,* a fictional tale about a boy who loves improving the world. "Ted is small, but he spends his days doing very big things," this picture book begins. On Sundays, Ted scrubs bottles for recycling. On Wednesdays, he walks dogs at the animal shelter. On Thursdays, he waters the garden. Ted has a sweet round face and pink circles on his cheeks. On Shabbat, the Jewish sabbath, he rests and dreams of *tikkun olam.* This book's illustrations, so cheerful, bright, and simple, had strangely carried me away, and I found myself imagining all the small ways our family could start helping our earth and our neighbors right away.

As the children continue drawing, Morah Elena tiptoes around the room in her leggings and fuzzy sweater, murmuring encouragement for their bright yellow suns, smiling stick figures, trees, and kittens and doggies. Jacob grins at me, his eyes gleaming. Whatever he hopes to see on my face is not there. Who knows what *is* there, what arrangement of features could possibly represent this unholy rainbow of feelings: shock, bewilderment, a full-body disappointment that won't stop growing. *Where* did he learn to write this? *What* does he mean by it? And *why* has he chosen this moment to share it, exposing flagrantly and publicly my maternal failings? For these, it feels, are what this paper announces most spectacularly at this moment, in this room, where I've come expressly as an adult emissary of my family's goodness.

On Monday, Ted makes inappropriate jokes. On Tuesday, he mocks the endeavors of well-meaning people.

Fumbling, I pull Jacob's paper from his hands and slip it into my bag. Did any of the other parents see? I scan the room. It appears not, but this brings little relief. It turns out it isn't fear of outside judgment that has seized me, but my own self-judgment, more caustic and piercing than another person's eyes could ever be. I know there are child development experts who believe in the power of nature over nurture, who would tell me my son is his own person, and that I'm no more responsible for his lapses than I am for his triumphs. But I've yet to meet a parent who can untangle their children from themselves this cleanly. In real time, on this real Sunday, my logic works more like this: Because I am a mother, I am the moral epicenter of my family's universe; my son's fissures must therefore ripple out from some primal fracture in me.

I glare at Jacob in a way that's meant to sink deep. My jaw is a hard dam, stanching what threatens to pour out. *We'll talk about this later,* I hiss. Later. In private. Far away from this cramped amphitheater of good men and women and their very good children, seeking to better the earth. A few feet away, a girl in a silver headband sketches herself raking leaves. Beautiful, bighearted, orange leaves that burst across the page like rising flames.

It's not too late, I think, to put this behind us. Probably, I'm taking this too seriously. Probably this is something he picked up from a first grade classmate, one with several sweaty older brothers and no limits, whom he's now imitating. He is only six. I pass him a fresh piece of paper and a handful of markers. His eyes narrow and his shoulders curl in like the edges of a shrinky-dink, but he grabs the paper from my hand, sullenly compliant, and then turns his hunched back to me and gets to work.

On my other side, Nora has drawn purple dashes above her garden. "What are those?" I ask hopefully, and she tells me they're a bird family. While the birds soar, thoughts descend on me like flies. I think about how we can never fully know our children's minds. I think about Freud and try to remember what I can about the phallic stage. But mostly, I think about how mothering my son so often feels like trying to steer a bike with a wobbly wheel: No matter how determined I am to aim the handlebars, we go crashing together off the curb again and again.

Jacob is finished with his new drawing. I ask to see it, but he demurs, covering it with the floppy arms of his sweatshirt, and I keep a respectful, and now wary, distance. Soon, the activity wraps up and the room begins to bustle. One of Jacob's friends comes over, and they start talking and giggling, and then they've turned their markers into knights' swords. The paper slips free from under my son's elbow.

A sea of white, two bobbing words at the center.

FEK MOMMY.

When I recount this incident to friends later, I turn it into a funny story, with all the character and color of a work of fiction. *There we were, in the middle of "repairing the world" day, and he's dropping F bombs on me!* I get laughs every time. With three kids and over a decade of experience as a mother, I'm practiced at the parental art of turning suffering to comedy. There's the time Nora had the flu and threw up all over me on the prescription pickup line at CVS— ha ha! And the time when, dizzy from lack of sleep, I took my colicky firstborn daughter out in the stroller, and it flipped over when the wheel hit a crack in the sidewalk. *There she was, hanging upside down like a cured ham*—he he! "Humor is just another defense against the universe," the comedian Mel Brooks once said. When it comes to parenting, it has felt like the most powerful defense I have against the orbit of crisis and rapture that is raising children.

But on the floor of my son's Hebrew school classroom, my insides crumple in a way that isn't funny at all. They crumple deep in my center, in the vast, quiet place where he spun into being, where his heart first quivered to life and his somersaults sent ripples across the flesh of my stomach so that I no longer knew where he ended and I began. I crumple because he's spun out into the world, turning and turning and turning—and because I can't seem to stop him from turning on me.

I love my son as I love all my children—which is to say, staggeringly, with an intensity that sometimes takes my breath away. When he emerged from my body and revealed that he was a boy, I was elated. We had our daughter Leigh then, and while I would have welcomed another healthy baby girl with joy and gratitude, I secretly thanked the universe for giving us this opportunity to parent a boy as well. I felt thankful in a very particular way for Paul, who lost his own father when he was seven, and who now had the chance to honor his dad's memory in perhaps the most cellular way possible—by being for his growing son all that his father had been for him. And I felt thankful that I could now experience what was by all accounts—or at least the accounts of my friends with male children—the uniquely tender bond that develops between a woman and her son. "There's just *something* between a boy and his mama," I remembered my friend Laura saying. Here was my chance to learn what this something was.

But from the very start, there's been nothing easeful or simple about the interplay between Jacob and me. I ought not—I know, I know—to compare my children, but the fact is there's an inevitable controlled experiment dynamic to parenting multiple kids, each one moving through the same stages of growth in more or less the same petri dish, announcing their differences whether we want them to or not. As infants, both of my daughters nursed calmly like painted cherubs, their tiny bodies nestled in the crook of my arm. Breastfeeding Jacob was more like a wrestling match, with him suddenly writhing and wailing at my breast until I lifted him away, and then writhing and wailing more furiously until I pulled him close again. Back and forth we'd go, his face growing redder, each round leaving me sweatier and more despairing than the last. If Paul were close by, I'd snap at him, enraged by his bodily freedom, and he would snap back, injured by my anger. If I could stay calm enough to remain pitiable, he would sometimes relieve me, gathering Jacob up and bouncing away with him to another room, shushing and shushing. It wasn't that Paul could always subdue him—but he could, somehow, weather his cries in a way that didn't feel to him intensely personal.

As he's grown from baby to toddler to little boy, Jacob and I have continued to wrestle. My daughters, too, have their moments of upset, of supermarket aisle meltdowns and late-day tantrums and pre-adolescent stomps across the kitchen floor. But with them, I can usually find some way to help restore equilibrium, whether through hugs or soothing words, distraction or minor bribery. My daughters have received and absorbed whatever comfort or per-spective I offer as a mother, unfolded and burgeoned in response, whereas Jacob seems slightly suspicious of it. The tools in my maternal storehouse so often bounce right off him, leaving me powerless to mother him. I'm reminded of the time his Lego heli-copter fell and broke, and he collapsed on the floor in a seething heap. I knew enough not to downplay this mishap, which would make him feel belittled; or to assure him we could rebuild the heli-copter, which would enrage him. So, on a whim, I kneeled down and shared with him something I often do when seized by strong emotions, which is to take three slow, deep breaths. "Do you want to try this with me?" I asked.

He covered his ears with his hands. "Stop talking to me about that yoga stuff!" he yelled.

Later that evening, as Paul and I cleaned up from dinner, I told him about this moment. "It's like he's impervious to strategy," I said. Paul listened, scrubbing away at a pan. Then he shrugged a little and laid the pan on a towel to dry. "He is who he is," he said, a response that in its understated mercy pretty much sums up why I married him.

It's time for Jacob's class to make the lasagna. Everyone shuffles with coats and bags toward the social hall, where the meal assembly will take place. My children and I make it as far as the classroom doorway, where I hold them back. I thrust Jacob's paper under his nose with too much feeling. It's the feeling not of a parent, controlled and centered, but of a person—a person who has been wronged and is now proffering proof of her injuries. "Does this say what I think it says?" I demand, my voice strained and tight, and then I say nothing. I don't scold or lecture or make him say "I'm sorry" because all of these require critical distance, which I don't have. At night, I've been reading *Peaceful Parent, Happy Kids*, a parenting manual about the importance of steadiness and calm. I'm supposed to be *mindful*, to make myself a tranquil sea where my son's pain can dissolve so he doesn't become a damaged and derelict adult. But at this moment, I don't care to feel peaceful, and it's not my son's happiness I'm after. What I'm feeling is wretched. What I want is to make him prove to me his goodness. Something in me will not rest until I've seen it displayed, until he's fulfilled this day's task. Because while there are all sorts of things I'm okay with my kids not being—star athletes or chess whizzes, budding maestros or spelling bee champions—I cannot abide their not being good.

On Wednesday, Ted ignores his teacher. On Thursday, he curses his mother.

"You hurt my feelings," I snap. "Look at me." I grab his chin. I do, I grab his chin. "Look at me. You've hurt my feelings."

Nora stands perfectly still. She turns to me, then to her brother, then back to me, her face smooth and satisfied in its innocence.

But Jacob won't look at me. I've never grabbed him like this before. He squeezes his eyes tight and claps his hands over his ears and pushes his body hard into the wall. His cheeks twist like wrung-out cloths and he turns his face to the ceiling and silently howls. And then he howls for real: a gush of anger and misery that seems intended to drown out its own noise. Some stragglers in the hallway turn and look, and I see that I've exposed something that doesn't belong here, that I must cover at once. I force my heart into a zone of peace. I open my arms and pull my son close with the strength of my deepest will. He squirms and pushes at me, and I lift him up and pull him to me tighter. The zipper of his sweatshirt pushes against my neck, toothed and cold. Slowly, his muscles ever-so-slightly ease, but not completely.

"Shhhh," I say, stroking the back of his head. "Shhhh." We end up, somehow, in a chair that's out in the hallway. I've subdued my own agitated self and have become again a mother, soft flesh and bosom, gold-haloed and serene. Nora trots over and clambers onto the other side of my lap, getting in on the goodness. There is too much weight on me, too much heat and skin, but this is the choice I've made. I lean my head back and allow myself to be covered.

· · ·

The concept of *tikkun olam* originates not in the Torah, the Hebrew bible, but in a creation myth envisioned by the sixteenth-century rabbi Isaac Luria, the father of the Jewish mystical tradition known as Kabbalah. I did not know this on Tikkun Olam Day, but learned it a few weeks later in a women's study group run by Rabbi Zecher. Six of my closest friends and I sat, as we do once a month, around a coffee table in her book-lined office. On this morning, we read Genesis, and she explained how Judaism actually contains several creation stories, all of them complementing one another. We all knew the version where God created the world in six days, and then rested on the seventh. And the version where God forms Adam out of clay, and Eve from Adam's rib. None of us knew Isaac Luria's version, which Rabbi Zecher described to us.

In everyday life, creating something—a building, a meal, a sculpture—is generally thought of as an act of external production. Here is the architect, the chef, the sculptor, and there, before her, is the thing she's made. In the Judeo-Christian tradition, the world's creation tends to be understood this way, too: On the one side there is God, and on the other there is the world God brings into being and then gazes upon, satisfied. Think of Michelangelo's *Creation of Adam* on the ceiling of the Sistine Chapel. Soaring and diaphanous, God reaches his finger toward Adam's naked, muscled form, as if he has sculpted this figure and is now, with divine power, animating it. Adam is *of* God, but Adam is not God.

But Luria, Rabbi Zecher explained, questioned this model of divine creation. If God is everywhere, he wondered, how can there be any space beyond God for creation to emerge? He envisioned an alternative origin story in which the world arises not through an act of production, but through *tsimtsum*, or an act of contraction. In the beginning, God's presence fills the universe. But then

God takes a breath and withdraws deeper into itself, creating a space for Earth and life to come into being, making *yesh* (something) from *ayin* (nothing). In this version of the world's beginning, God does not so much impose or demand, but pull back and allow. The word *tsimtsum*, so mysterious and peculiar, felt familiar. Finally, I remembered that this was the name, in Yann Martel's *Life of Pi*, of the Japanese freighter that sinks on its passage across the Pacific, leaving the adolescent Pi stranded with a tiger on a lifeboat. I'd taught this book many times to my high school students, never quite seeing, as I did now, the connection between this swallowed ship and Pi's spiritual growth as he rises, orphaned, to the demands of nine solitary months on a boundless ocean.

But I do not yet have Luria or Martel to think of as we stand at our lasagna-making station. I'm just determined to get the rest of this morning right. The air is sour with tomato sauce, and around us spoons clink and bags of shredded cheese rip as the children follow their instructions. Nora's eyes brighten as I lift her onto the counter and help her pry open a tub of ricotta—she loves messy projects. But Jacob sits on the floor, rigid and brooding. Once again, he will not do what I want him to do.

The fact that my children's tendencies align perfectly with gender stereotypes—my girls conscientious and people-pleasing, my boy willful and devil-may-care—isn't lost on me. It only makes me strain more aggressively for things to be otherwise. Is this alignment just coincidence? In what unconscious, unspoken ways might my children's community, their teachers, their schools— might *my husband and I*—have steered our children toward these gendered ways of being? At a time when "toxic masculinity" has become a household phrase, there's widespread understanding for the first time of the consequences of raising girls to toe the line, and boys to flout it. I've long been a feminist and a champion of gender equality, but as a mother during this time in history, I feel this calling in a new and intimate way. The lessons of our era hover, always, in my mind, reminding me that my son will become a man, and that what I impart to him in the interim in crucial. I want all my children, of course, to be empathic and kind, decent and honorable. But what I long for most pressingly—what it feels my work hinges on—is to raise a good son.

On Friday, Ted imposes his will. On Saturday, he acts on his urges.

In our aluminum tray, the lasagna grows. Nora's lips pucker with concentration as she scoops sauce from a jar and spreads it with the back of her spoon. On and on she goes, scooping and spreading, layering and admiring. Another parent engages me in small talk, and I follow the script as best I can. But everywhere I look, slabs of noodles are being slathered in sauce and sprinkled with fluffy handfuls of mozzarella—offerings of care and nourishment in which my boy will have no part.

Finally, we're released. We pick up Leigh from her classroom, and then I pile the kids into the car and drive the half hour to my sister-in-law Jacqui's house. My niece opens the door in a unicorn headdress, and the four cousins go thumping upstairs together to play.

I have come to Jacqui's because she's my go-to partner in commiseration, my favorite person to turn to in unhappy times. Whatever I tell her, I can count on her to be unshaken, or to outdo me with a worse tale of woe. I lie down on her couch and tell her about my morning while she clears lunch dishes and feeds the dog scraps. I don't sugarcoat or mine my experience for laughs. I don't say, "This might sound funny on the surface, but..."

What I say on that dog hair–covered couch, on the sagging end of that tired mothering weekend, is that I have lost myself. I have lost myself in becoming a mother, and I feel I can't project with any truth what I'm, of course, supposed to project, which is that the sacrifices have all been worth it. I've loved and given and toiled and grieved as a mother. I've run marathons that ended in new marathons, and then I've run onward until I've collapsed. I've tapped into reserves of energy I never knew existed, and I've siphoned away these reserves, drilling down deeper for more. I know I should rise above the challenges that come my way, for this is what mothers—the world's anointed absorbers of pain—must do. But I cannot rise above my son's *fuck you.*

Jacqui finishes loading the dishwasher and then looks at me, toweling off her hands, her face unchanged.

"So he got angry at you for ruining his penis joke?" she says.

"Well, yeah," I say.

"And to deal with that anger, he expressed his feelings on paper, in writing?" she says.

"I guess."

"Even though he has a language delay, and gets Early Intervention, and writing is hard for him?" she says. "He didn't yell or scream?"

I don't say anything.

"That's a fucking awesome parenting success story, if you ask me," she says, and then she sits down on the couch next to me and reaches for the remote control. Outside the window, the barren

March afternoon darkens to evening. Inside, the television blooms neon, illuminating Jacqui's face in joyous flashes.

I'm beginning to see how I've gotten this day all wrong.

In Luria's creation myth, something wild and bizarre happens after God contracts, something out of a science-fiction movie. Divine light enters the newly formed darkness, carried there in ten sacred vessels—like a fleet of rockets rising through a cinematic sky. But some of these vessels are too fragile to contain God's light, and they burst and shatter, scattering divine sparks across the world. Luria proposes that if our world is imperfect—if there is evil and injustice and heartache and anguish—it's because of this *shevirah*, this breaking of the vessels, the cosmic accident that thwarted God's plan for us all.

In contemporary Judaism, this idea is at the root of *tikkun olam*. It's through acts of restoration, or *tikkun*, that the world, our *olam*, can be brought closer to the divine wholeness God intended for it. Through *tikkun olam* big and small—from sidestepping an ant in your path to marching twenty miles to protest injustice—humans can become God's co-creators, each of us doing our part to heal the world's fractures.

I love the image of the vessels, so beautiful in their peculiar specificity. And I take comfort in the idea of *tikkun olam* because of its emphasis on action. As a Jew, I am not charged with regular repentance—though often, repenting is what I know I must do. Self-punishment isn't my main task, either, although I reproach myself hourly. My main task is to enter each moment looking for the good choice to make, the generous action to take, gathering whatever scattered sparks I see.

My children's sparks are everywhere—on the floor, the stairs, the rug. They accumulate in corners and under tables. They trail their bodies like crumbs. The more I train my eyes to see them, the harder it becomes to lose sight of their light. What more can I do but collect them in my hands, holding them up for my children to see? What more can I say but "Here, here is your goodness. Look how brightly it glows."

We're home. Paul has returned from his trip, and there's balance again in the house, a lightening in my step at the sight of his bags flung down in the entryway. I want to unburden myself, to tell him everything, but this will have to wait until the kids are asleep. For now, it's enough to have him here, his presence alone making my earlier angst feel dreamlike and alien. As we clean up the dinner mess and coax the children upstairs for baths and toothbrushing, I settle back comfortably into partnership. One of us will put the two girls to bed, and one of us, our son. I take my son.

Jacob's room waits for us—his bed with the checkered comforter, the dresser covered in Legos, the splashes of Pokémon cards on the rug, the overturned beanbag chair. After I read him two picture books, after I pull down his shades and fill his water cup and turn on the white noise of his sound machine, I gather the far-flung pieces of myself and climb into bed with him in the dark.

"This morning, at Hebrew school, you felt upset with me for taking your paper away," I say.

He does not respond.

"I'm *glad* you love all the parts of yourself," I say. "You should! All of you is beautiful and special. And in a way, that note was also kind of funny. I didn't see the funniness earlier because I was too mad. I was mad you weren't doing what you were told to."

His face tilts in my direction. Light from the street slips through the crack in his shade, making diamond patterns on the wall.

"But I think there are better ways for people to show anger than I did, kinder ways than snatching things away, or using harsh and ugly words. Don't you think?"

His comforter rustles as he turns onto his belly, and I know—because I am his mother—that he hears what I'm saying. I say it out loud anyway.

"I wish I had shown my anger better. I love you so much, baby boy. And I'm sorry."

I feel for my son's hand and squeeze it tight. He wriggles in closer, nudging his head into the space above my shoulder. The white noise whirs. I can feel his hair on my neck, as damp and matted as the day he was born—that April day six years ago, when I took a breath, contracted, and he came to life.

Now, again, I contract, holding back my power and my will, leaving room for him to rise into this moment in his own way, to make of this space his own creation.

Ted holds his mother's cheeks between his hands. Ted kisses one side of her face, and then the other. Ted locks his body around her like a magnet, like a clasp.

There will be time, maybe tomorrow, to rake the leaves. There will be time for buying a compost bin and walking the dogs at the shelter and watering the plants. But tonight, we lie on the bed looking up at the ceiling. We watch the splinters of light rising up like stars, and we do our imperfect best to repair the world.

A Place, or a State
of Affairs

This crescent of Cape Cod beach, down a dirt road from the cottage Paul and I are staying in for the weekend, is nearly empty. Waves slosh against the pebbled shore. The clouds, when they pass, take their time, drifting in languorous wisps. In my lap are a notebook and Thoreau's *Walden*, which I'll be teaching this fall in my eleventh grade American literature class.

I read some paragraphs—watch foam swirling around rocks, a mother pulling a child through the water on a boogie board—and contemplate how I'll make Thoreau matter to a room of twenty-first-century teenagers. It's been years since I read *Walden* in my own high school English class. Was it Thoreau, or was it Emerson, who wrote about following your own drumbeat? I scan the pages, searching. "If a man does not keep pace with his companions, perhaps it is because he hears a different drummer." *Yes*. I underline this sentence, remembering how it sung to me when I was seventeen, and feeling so chronically off-tempo.

Paul has gone fishing for the morning, but I'm not technically, in this moment, alone. Under my cotton cover-up, beneath the stretched fibers of my bathing suit, below the rounded skin of my belly, is our first child. She has been inside me for sixteen weeks

154

now. Recently, I've started to feel her: She is the nudge of a row-boat against a dock, the ripple of seaweed in water. But mostly, she is still. I can read for long stretches, burying my feet, feeling little pyramids of sand spill from my toes as I lift them out again, and forget entirely that she's with me.

I look up from my book. There, again, are the mother and child. She's a young mother, stout and athletic, and her child is maybe three or four—a girl. She lies belly-down on her boogie board, kicking and paddling. But this effort is pure pretend. It's the mother who pulls her through the water, her face immobile, her wrist through the loop of the cord, her calves stamping through surf as she moves from left to right across my field of vision.

I can feel my energy waning, as it has so easily since I've been pregnant. I tip my head back against my beach chair. When I get back to the house, I think, I'll make myself a toasted cheese. Or maybe a tuna sandwich? Seagulls squawk and the August sun glides over my legs. It's possible I fall asleep.

When I open my eyes: mother and child, moving from right to left. Trudge, trudge go the mother's legs; paddle, paddle go her daughter's hands. How long, I think, can this go on? The mother hauls her daughter all the way down to the jetty, and then back they come, rope taut, board bouncing, the mother's gaze in front of her. The girl is happy, chattering. The mother is—I cannot tell what the mother is. Devoted, clearly. But devotion isn't exactly an emotion.

Do I have the sense, as I watch this woman, that I am seeing into my future? Or is it only later, after our daughter is born, and then our son, and then our younger daughter—when our floor-boards bang with feet, and our walls climb with toys, and from upstairs or the next room or the rug at my feet a child is calling

155

Mama, Mama, come here Mama, watch Mama, open this Mama, Mama, Mama, Mama, Mama—that this memory starts to shimmer like an omen. The sand, the clouds, the water. Thoreau in his wooded hermitage. The boogie board, the rope. The mother with her shackled wrist, trailing a child behind her.

When our daughter is born, my husband cuts the cord, but there are other yokes between us. I know from reading my baby manuals that newborns arrive ready to feed, but nothing has prepared me for the sheer animal force of my daughter's appetite, the damp insistence of her body, rooting at my bare chest in search of nourishment. As I watch her mouth lock onto my breast, as I feel the rhythmic tug of her sucking and my body's dormant powers stirring awake, I understand she has only partly loosed herself from me. I look at Paul and begin to cry. My daughter is in me and I am in her, and I cannot tell where she ends and I begin.

If only awe were sustainable and I could tap, perpetually, into this sublime togetherness. But by the time we're home from the hospital, something in me has shifted. Before, when breastfeeding was a picturesque activity I occasionally glimpsed on planes and park benches, it had seemed like a brief and pleasant respite in a woman's day. I'm stunned to discover how long a feeding takes: twenty minutes on one side, followed by twenty on the other. Newborns, the postpartum nurse informs me, eat every two hours, which seems half-reasonable until I learn the clock resets at the *start*, not the end, of each feeding. A new mother spends a third of her day with a body in her arms, a mouth on her skin, her baby's heat and hunger pinning her down.

My husband is not pinned down. He's so good, so helpful, with his mobility. He hustles to fetch me burp cloths, glasses of water, slices of toast. How, I wonder, do so many women do this alone—women without eager partners, or partners at all? Then, two weeks later, his paternity leave ends. He heads out the door and does not return until my sweatpants are sagging and the evening news is flashing, and I am not sure where my day or life has gone.

What's hardest about these hours isn't the breastfeeding, or cycles of laundry, or on-and-off of diapers, or even the urgent *na na na!* of my daughter's cries. It's the way these things together fill all time and space, spreading into the corners of our little apartment, rising to my knees, thighs, groin, and then up under my ribcage, until something essential inside me has been crowded out. My aunt calls to talk, but the baby is fussing. I need to pee, but the baby is spitting up. The moment I follow the trail of my own longings—reaching for a book, or sinking into thought as I stare at the flowered couch pillows—I am jerked backward, my daughter's needs yanking me from myself.

There are products to help with this, bouncers and swings and an egg-shaped contraption called a Mamaroo I nearly buy that mimics the movements of the womb. But in the middle-class child-raising culture of which I'm now part, a culture lorded over by Dr. William Sears and other attachment parenting theorists, these aids are all a little suspect—corner-cutting and possibly baby-ruining substitutes for the very best bouncing, swinging, shushing thing, which is me. Nothing, Dr. Sears warns in *The Baby Book*, can replace the ministrations of an ever-present mother, so attuned to her baby's gestures that she can respond to them immediately, laying the groundwork for a happy life. And so I buy products that bind my daughter and me closer: a sling that hangs from my neck so I can wear her, a bassinet that affixes to my bedside so I can sleep with her, a monitor that clips to my waistband when I slip out for the mail. The cords between us are wireless, or cotton, or nylon with plastic buckles. They wind around our bodies and click snugly into place, fastening us together.

My daughter is so beautiful, so perfect, with palms that curl like little moons. Her smile is a window into the hugeness of the world. And yet it's not easy for me, all this she-and-I-ness, the constant relational orbit that is our life. How many times, when I was pregnant, had I been warned about the isolation of being home with a baby? *Join a moms' group! Make time to connect with friends!* But it's not communion I lack, or loneliness I feel. I cannot yet name what I feel—even to myself.

When my maternity leave ends, I leave my teaching job, which I love, and accept a work-from-home curriculum-writing job, which I do not love, so I can remain with my baby as much as possible. How can I *not*, I think—as many American mothers doing the grim math have thought—given that my salary would just barely cover the cost of childcare? I count myself lucky to have found a way to both work and be with our child, and when I tell people so, I'm not lying. For I've never loved anything as intensely as I love our daughter, who has moons for hands, and the world in her smile— and from whom part of me longs just as intensely to flee.

Thoreau devotes a full chapter of *Walden* to the allure of solitude, describing the pleasure of escaping the "wearisome and dissipating" company of others and entering into deeper communion with the self. "Not till we are lost—in other words, not till we have lost the world—do we begin to find ourselves," he reflects.

In his quest to "lose the world," Thoreau was following the long line of real and fictional retreaters and "rugged individuals" who have shaped America's cultural psyche. When Daniel Boone ventured into the frontier wilderness; when Huck Finn escaped from his "sivilizing" guardians and "lit out" on the Mississippi; when Ishmael set sail aboard the *Pequot* onto the "mystical ocean"—each, in his way, was heeding the call of solitude. Aloneness permeates the poetry of Walt Whitman, where freedom of the self is achieved not through solitary adventure but leisurely solitary reverie. "I loaf and invite my soul / I lean and loaf at my ease… observing a spear of summer grass," begins "Song of Myself."

The twentieth century produced a new solitary hero, the cool and distanced outsider: James Dean, following his own drumbeat in a leather jacket, and Johnny Cash in head-to-toe black crooning, "I'll be what I am. A solitary man." And it produced a fresh crop of wilderness escapists, like Christopher McCandless, whose Jack London–inspired retreat into the Alaska backwoods was captured in Jon Krakauer's *Into the Wild*. Not to mention Krakauer himself, who describes in this same book the impulse that has lured *him*, over and over, up the world's tallest mountains.

Since becoming a mother, I've become driven, almost obsessively, to grasp what, precisely, solitude *is*, so that I might understand why I crave it so voraciously. I've tunneled into the work of experts, such as philosopher Philip J. Koch, who suggests that while relationship offers its own gifts, only alone can we experience certain restorative virtues. Solitude allows "freedom of action," the leeway to fill each moment authentically and spontaneously, released from others' demands. It awakens our creativity. It provides the pause we need to achieve "reflective perspective," that deeper understanding of the experiences that bombard us. In *The*

Call of Solitude, psychologist Ester Schaler Buchholz maintains that time alone isn't just a virtue but a deep human need with origins in the womb. The calm, contained safety in which we awakened into consciousness is stamped onto our psyches, beckoning us home. Fulfilling "our wishes to explore, our curiosity about the unknown, our desires to escape from another's control, our will to be an individual," solitude, she argues, is the very "fuel for life."

When I was seventeen, sitting in Mr. O'Connor's American Literature class discussing Thoreau and Whitman, drawing asterisks in my books with chipped-polish fingers, writing five-paragraph essays on solitary contemplation, it never occurred to me that these writers' sacred space could not forever be my sacred space, or their life fuel, my fuel. When I was in my twenties and thirties, leading class discussions of Emerson and Melville, assigning essays on self-sovereignty and wanderlust, it never occurred to me that these authors' journeys could not be *all* my students' journeys, or their discoveries, *all* my students' discoveries.

Only after I've had children does it hit me that the solitary seekers who forged the pathways of my imagination, shaping my understanding of a life well lived, of human destiny, of *my* destiny, were all men. Only after I've had children do I realize that motherhood and selfhood might be entirely incompatible callings.

"The first year is the hardest," people say. And in ways, they're right. The nursing wanes; the straps of the sling loosen once and for all. But always, there are new cords binding me to my daughter, and then her brother, and later their sister. The cord is my worry, pulling me after each sprinting toddler. The cord is my arm, gathering up each tired preschooler. The cord is our schedule, with its flurry of appointments and commitments. The cord is my guilt, insisting, always, there's more of myself I could be giving, tugging me home when I've lingered too long on an errand, or strayed too far on a run, even as the sky above me pulses orange and the dusk air is like a cold drink in my throat. Time, once I'm a mother, is never fully my own. It is pooled time, communal time. When I seize it for myself, it is stolen time.

"A man is rich in proportion to the number of things which he can afford to let alone," wrote Thoreau. What does this mean for mothers, I wonder, who are increasingly expected—even as fathers are more involved than ever—to leave *nothing* alone when it comes to their families? In her landmark 1989 book *The Second Shift*, sociologist Arlie Hochschild revealed that mothers, even when employed, spent at least twice as much time as fathers on housework and childcare—a statistic that still holds true. And while it's easy to think of Betty Friedan's "happy housewife heroine," confined to hearth and home, as an emblem of a bygone era, American mothers today actually spend *more* time—nearly double—caring for children than they did in the 1960s.

This care work has also intensified. Tending to kids once meant ushering them outside to play unsupervised, or plopping them for long stretches in front of cartoons. I rarely played with my own mother as a child, except the occasional game of Mastermind or Old Maid. Instead, I ventured on long walks with the dog. I slipped a dollar in my pocket and strolled to the convenience store to buy Fun Dip.

Now, more often, tending to children means sustained, mutual engagement in hands-on activities: reading, crafting, baking, practicing sports, doing STEM projects. A 2019 study revealed that this extreme child-rearing style has become the standard not only for the upper-middle-class "helicopter" parents who can most easily afford it but for American parents generally, regardless of income, education, or race.

To make room for all this child-centered togetherness, something needs to give—and what has given, overwhelmingly, is mothers' autonomous time. Between 1975 and 2000, mothers' time to themselves dropped by seven hours a week. By 2011, according to a paper in the *American Sociological Review*, American mothers had approximately thirty-six minutes a day to themselves. A 2008 study revealed that most mothers' uninterrupted time lasts, on average, no more than ten minutes at a stretch. In the early months of the COVID-19 pandemic and its attendant school closures, those ten minutes, one mother reported in the *Washington Post*, shrank to less than four.

Three minutes and twenty-four seconds, give or take.

One evening when our kids are eight, five, and three—after my husband and I have herded everyone upstairs and tickled their arms and read them *one last story please*—I burrow into bed and belatedly listen to a voicemail. It's Jessica, one of my oldest friends, telling me in her gentle way that she's hurt I haven't returned her call from yesterday. Am I okay? I feel bad that I've let her down, that I've been a negligent friend. I am bone-tired, the kind of tired that makes even speaking hard, but I call her back. "I'm so sorry," I say. "It's been crazy with the kids and I haven't had a window." I can sense, as these words leave my mouth, how disingenuous they sound, so disingenuous that I suspect myself of lying. Really? No window at all?

But it *is* true: no window. Fragments, shards, scattered splinters of time and space, yes. But nothing expansive enough to make meaning with. My remorse morphs into frustration. Jessica doesn't understand what it's like, I think, because she doesn't have children. And then I have a thought that's been nagging at me lately—gathering, mounting—which is that what it's *truly* like, hour to hour, minute to minute, to be a mother, isn't something frequently exposed in its purest form, and therefore, I suspect, not generally understood. I did not, before I had children, understand it, and so I've spent the past eight years wondering why *no one told me* about this relentless quotidian frenzy, this near-perpetual geyser of frenzy that cannot be stanched. A few years later while listening to a podcast, I will encounter for the first time the German word *zerrissenheit*, which is sometimes translated as "torn-to-pieces-hood," and I will think, *thank god. Thank god* I finally have the vocabulary to describe this geyser that won't stop erupting, blasting me every day into thousands of far-flung pieces.

There are times, and this moment on the phone is one of them, when I wish I had video footage of a typical day with my children so that I could simply press *play* and say, "Here. Here is what I mean."

I might cue up, for starters, the very day that was just now ending—an unremarkable Friday in February. I'd headed with Nora to pick up her siblings at school, and as we arrived home, snow began falling. I envisioned the cozy afternoon we'd have together, drinking cocoa and making Valentines. As they got to work with their glue and doilies, I thought, *I should post a photo of this on Instagram!* It was just the sort of harmonious family tableau Instagram loves. But I never actually took this photo, because the moment I turned on the stove, our kitchen became a triage area, frenetic with needs. Leigh wanted three scoops of chocolate powder in her mug. Jacob wanted two, but each from a different brand. Nora, once hers had been poured, decided she didn't want cocoa after all, but raspberry tea. She marched her mug to the sink in protest, trailing milky splatters that I couldn't wipe up because Jacob was calling me over, beseechingly, *now*, to examine a papercut, uncap a pen. And then Leigh: to find a scissor, spell a word. At some point, a fight broke out, and I quelled it. As sparkles spilled and paper clippings fell to the floor, stomachs grew hungry. I brought over bowls of pretzels, and then asked the kids to clear their emptied bowls, and then asked so many times that the asks became yells, and then the yells coalesced into a single, guttural howl. Jacob began to cry, because he is exquisitely sensitive, and because truly, I shouldn't howl at my children. I wanted to talk with them about this, to redeem myself, to *debrief*. But I saw on the microwave clock that it was closing in on dinner time—and there were still baths to do—so instead I grabbed green beans from the fridge and started furiously snapping off the ends, furious at myself, furious at my kids for making me furious with myself. My legs throbbed and the corners of my eyes burned with anger and shame, and suddenly, I felt so cramped, so hot, and I realized that I still hadn't taken off my jacket.

There was a time when I would have made from this episode a redemptive story. I would have known the exact moment in the denouement where I was meant to summon beauty, and I would have summoned it. I would have said, *Sure, mothering can be hard, but it all goes so fast! And seeing my kids' heart-shaped doily creations lying cheerfully on the counter that evening reminded me how the magic makes everything worth it.*

I don't say things like this anymore. More often now, I say things like "Why do I live hundreds of miles from my mother?" and "Humans were meant to live in kinship clans!" and "The nuclear family has been terrible for women" and "This country needs quality, affordable childcare." But even my most plaintive cries land, on my own ears, like whispers—too soft, too vague, to capture what simmers below the surface of my maternal skin.

"Anger," suggests Ester Schaler Buchholz, "may simply be the alone need asserting itself the only way it can."

In the canonical works I read in high school—and later imparted to a new generation of teenage girls and boys—there may have been no women "lighting out" on solo adventures. But there were, here and there, women alone in rooms, retreating into a more bounded and domestic version of solitude. There was Emily Dickinson, stowed away in her Amherst home, penning poem after poem, some of which conjured the transcendent power of aloneness. There was Virginia Woolf, writing—presumably in her own room—about the necessity of "a room of one's own" for any woman who wishes "to set free whatever is in the brain." By this, she meant not just a literal room but the psychic space to pursue her thoughts as they unspool toward insight, or weave themselves, unbroken, into pattern.

In her essay "On Being Alone," Elizabeth Bishop writes: "It is as if being with people were the Earth of the mind,...but in being alone, the mind finds its Sea, the wide quiet plane with different lights in the sky and different, more secret sounds." And poet May Sarton focuses a whole book on the topic, *Journal of a Solitude*, in which she chronicles a yearlong retreat to her New Hampshire house. "What is strange," she muses as she settles into her seclusion, is "that friends, even passionate love, are not my real life unless there is time alone in which to explore and to discover what is happening or what has happened." Bishop and Sarton highlight an important aspect of solitude, which is how it works in tandem with togetherness. Aloneness isn't a superior state to companionship but its counterbalance, and it's in the reconciliation of these opposites that wholeness can emerge.

In the twenty-first century, the solitary female adventurer has finally arrived as a literary trope. She has ventured out of the home, becoming more peripatetic and courageous—more stereotypically male. I'm thinking, for instance, of Elizabeth Gilbert, who in her memoir *Eat Pray Love* recounts setting out alone through Italy, India, and Indonesia. And of Cheryl Strayed, who in *Wild* describes trekking solo across hundreds of miles of the Pacific Crest Trail. "Alone," Strayed reflects, "had always felt like an actual place, . . . a room where I could retreat to be who I really was." Out in the wilderness, "Alone wasn't a room anymore, but the whole wide world, and now I was alone in that world, occupying it in a way I never had before." For Strayed, the walls of Woolf's metaphoric room have cracked wide open, solitude pouring to the horizon.

Is it a coincidence that neither Dickinson nor Woolf nor Bishop nor Sarton nor Gilbert nor Strayed (when she set out on her journey) had children? I don't think so. It is one thing for Odysseus to leave Penelope and Telemachus back in Ithaca as he sails for decades upon the wine-dark sea. But mothers have never been able to assert their alone needs quite so easily in life or literature—at least not without negative, and often devastating, consequences.

Edna Pontellier, the heroine of Kate Chopin's *The Awakening*, stands as a classic example of the fate that can befall a mother who claims too much space for herself. During a seaside vacation with her children, Edna tastes true freedom as she begins to defy the obligations of the good Victorian mother and wife, discovering— through solitude and artistic expression—the depths of her own personhood. But motherhood and personhood prove irreconcilable for Edna, who, increasingly alienated by her community, can see no way out of her predicament other than through suicide. The book ends with Edna standing at the ocean's edge, visions of her children appearing in her mind's eye "like antagonists who had overcome her." The sea calls to her, "whispering, clamoring, murmuring, inviting the soul to wander in abysses of solitude," and she steps forth, giving herself over to this last hope for inner freedom.

A similar doom awaits Susan Rawlings, the protagonist of Doris Lessing's 1963 story "To Room Nineteen." A married mother of four, Susan lives a seemingly idyllic life with her family in their large country home. But inside, she's restless, hounded by a nameless longing. Slowly, she identifies the root of her problem: a lack of privacy. "Not for one moment in twelve years have I been alone, had time to myself," she realizes. Even when she can isolate herself physically, the children "would be in the next room, or waiting for her to do something for them; or it would soon be time for lunch or tea, or to take one of them to the dentist." She begins to understand that true solitude will require more than removing herself from the corporal presence of others. It will require:

> A place, or a state of affairs, where it would not be necessary to keep reminding herself: In ten minutes I must telephone Jacob about…and at half past three I must leave early for the children because the car needs cleaning….[N]ever, not for one second, ever, was she free from the pressure of time, from having to remember this or that. She could never…let herself go into forgetfulness.

Sociologists, in 1963, had not yet coined the terms "invisible labor" or "mental load" to describe the unseen planning and organizing and managing that women do, nearly constantly, to keep their children thriving and their households running. But these are exactly what Lessing conjures here.

For example, my husband takes our daughter Nora to a birthday party. He is present, involved, sharing in the childcare. What the world doesn't see are the behind-the-scenes orchestrations that have made this moment possible: fielding the invitation, RSVP-ing, selecting and purchasing the gift, making sure Nora's party clothes are out of the laundry in time, cajoling her to the kitchen table to make a card. These things I have done—not exactly by design but by a sort of gendered default that Paul and I, like so many previously egalitarian married couples, slipped into in spite of ourselves when we became parents, the way a wheel slips into a well-rutted groove.

To escape this invisible freight, in "To Room Nineteen," Susan takes over a spare room at the top of the house and then secretly rents a room for a few hours in a small hotel. This retreat is so delicious, so deeply what she needs, that she convinces her husband, without revealing exactly why, that they should hire an au pair. One hotel visit becomes three visits a week, and then five, and life gets better and better for Susan until her forbearing husband—understandably suspicious she's having an affair—hires a detective to follow her, ruining everything.

Here's the part of the story that always gets me. Rather than disclosing to her husband that she's been spending these hours alone, Susan allows him to persist in believing she has *taken a lover*. She even invents a name for this lover (Michael) and a profession (publisher), the lies rolling off her tongue faster than she can conceive of the problem she's causing herself. She seems to grasp that the desire for solitude in a mother is so deviant, so taboo, that even carnal desire would be better for her to admit to. She protects her husband from a betrayal more perverse than an affair with another man: an affair with her autonomous self.

But of course, there is no Michael. And no clear way for the swiftly unraveling Susan to keep hold of her tenuous selfhood. And so, like Edna, she commits suicide—fittingly, in her beloved hotel room, as if through death she might preserve her wholeness forever.

These are some of the places I've found solitude as a mother: Behind the wall of our living room, while the kids play unaware on the other side. On the far end of our porch, tucked out of view from the window. In the dawn embrace of my bedroom, pretending, when the first small fingers slip through the door crack, that I'm fast asleep. I've escaped from my children to the cool, white calm of a locked bathroom, flushing the toilet for cover before I emerge. And to the side of the road down the street from our house, where I've gazed at the heavens through my sunroof while the groceries wilted.

I've found ways to be alone even when I most appear not to be. When I'm, say, snuggling on the couch with my children, reading them a book. How connected we look! A big happy tangle of elbows and socks and hair. They do not know, as I turn each page, that I am somewhere else, that each sentence I utter is a decoy to hold their attention so I can wriggle out from under it. *What did the bear mean, Mama, when he said that about the parachute?* I have no idea what he meant, for I was not there. I was at the edge of the ocean, the top of a mountain, the outskirts of the Milky Way, swimming in stardust.

I've found solace as a mother in the soft narcotic light of a dentist's chair, and in a curtained corner of Beth Israel hospital's emergency room after smacking my head—while racing to clean up after a slime-making project—on the underside of our granite counter. Once it was clear that I was going to be okay, I didn't want to leave that hospital, and it wasn't the hypnotic murmur of a slow ER morning or the blanketed stillness of my gurney that I clung to as much as my utter clarity—due to the rivulets of dried blood on my neck, and the discharge papers that hadn't yet arrived—that there was no one I was supposed to be with at that moment but myself.

Without this clarity, solitude can hardly be called solitude, for it is rotted by doubt. Shouldn't I prefer fluffing egg whites for meringues with Leigh, or watching Jacob's new magic trick, or wrapping Nora in a towel like a burrito as I pretend to eat her nose, to sitting alone in a parked car with the window open, watching my arm hairs stiffen in the breeze?

Isolation, alienation, loneliness—these are the forms of aloneness we fear, solitude's dreaded step-siblings. But the truth is I rarely feel lonely when I'm by myself. What has felt lonely, unbearably lonely, is harboring in silence my suspicion that I'm the most flawed and compromised mother walking the earth, with my recurring urges to flee what I most love.

It is reading—my whole life, it has been reading—that lifts me out of this cramped, lonely place. As I read more about the human urge for separateness, I eventually begin to talk a little about the problem of mothers and solitude. I give this problem my own official-sounding name—"maternal solitude deficit"—and I float my theories out to one friend, and then another. What happens is magnificent: Their eyes glint with recognition; they throw their heads back in knowing laughter; they tell me their mother secrets. Mira hides in her home office, pretending to be working. Laura invents urgent reasons to head to the grocery store. Michelle leaves for appointments a half hour too early, winding aimlessly in her car over mute back roads.

One morning, on the phone with my mother, I run my theories by her, too. Did she ever long for escape when my brother and I were kids? I can't recall ever sensing she was chafing against our presence. "Oh, yes!" she says. "Sometimes I would sneak into my bedroom after I got home from work so I could be by myself before you two saw me. I just needed that space, that time."

Mothers' smuggled moments of solitude might be the best-kept secret of our era.

And yet, still, there's a risk I take in writing this essay, a question skulking under its belly like a shadow on the sea floor, and that question is this: "If you yearn so deeply for solitude, is it possible you shouldn't have had children?" I have asked myself this very question at times, and the asking has been like a riptide through my blood.

But slowly, I've come to appreciate this question, as one appreciates useful things, because I see how perfectly it encapsulates the central problem of motherhood as an institution, which is its failure of nuance, its relentless oversimplification, its devotion to binary. Either you adore your children or you do not; either you enjoy mothering or you do not; either you were meant to be a mother or you clearly, decidedly—monstrously—were not.

Every day, I must draw on my deepest resources to take a stand against this question that towers over me like a monolith, leaving me shrinking from my own complexity. Because, in the end, isn't it *complexity* that Edna and Susan and my friends and I yearn to reclaim for ourselves when we abscond from our families? Longing for escape doesn't make a mother bad: It makes her a person, because to be a person is to be home to a million competing impulses and incongruities. Men have understood and embraced this fact for ages. "A foolish consistency is the hobgoblin of little minds," wrote Emerson, adding this encouragement to anyone worried inconsistency might lead others to misjudge them: "Is it so bad, then, to be misunderstood? Pythagoras was misunderstood, and Socrates, and Jesus, and Luther, and Copernicus, and Galileo, and Newton, and every pure and wise spirit that ever took flesh. To be great is to be misunderstood." In "Song of Myself," Whitman similarly owns up to his own internal paradoxes—boasts about them, really: "Do I contradict myself? / Very well then I contradict myself, / (I am large, I contain multitudes.)" Women have rarely been able to claim such multiplicity—and mothers, perhaps, least of all.

Do I savor examining the crenelated edges of a horseshoe crab with Jacob and also long to take off down the beach without him? Do I thrill at the sight of Nora's face as I move up the carpool line and also wish the school day were two hours longer? Do I cherish lying in the past-bedtime dark with Leigh and also silently hope she will *go to sleep already*?

Very well, then. I savor and long. Thrill and wish. Cherish and hope away.

I contain multitudes.

• • •

It's a Sunday morning, and I'm home alone with Nora. I rarely have time with just one child, and I clear the breakfast table as quickly as I can, determined to give my daughter my full attention.

When I call for her, there's no answer. Then I hear her—talking to someone? I follow her voice to the living room, where she's tucked between a chair and the edge of the bookshelf. She has a stuffed badger in one hand and a stuffed seal in the other, and she's conversing with them—or rather, through them—in a language that's both English and not English. I can grasp each individual word but not her sentences, which follow the rules of a mysterious private syntax originating deep within her.

"Want to play something together?" I ask. "Hi-Ho Cherry-O? Or make necklaces with the beads we bought the other day?"

"Maybe later," she murmurs, dancing her stuffies across her lap.

I kneel down next to her, looking for a way into her game. "Why is the badger on his head?"

"Because," she says, "he's diving into the Atlantic Ocean."

"And the seal? The seal is planning to join him?"

"Of *course* not," she sighs. "He's getting ready to judge the race."

"Ah!" I say. And then don't know what to say, for we seem to have reached an impasse. I sit beside her, until her hands grow still and she looks at me. She seems to be considering something, weighing something.

"Sometimes I like to play alone, Mama," she says. And then, tentatively, "Can I play alone?"

My daughter, at the age of five, can't possibly fathom the meaning I hear in these words, or how they wash over me like revelation.

I cannot snap my fingers and create the conditions that would give legions of mothers more space for pause. I cannot single-handedly reverse the geographical trends that have left so many parents isolated from extended family, or enact legislation that would enable affordable, high-quality childcare, or change the fact that US tax policy is still designed to benefit households with one earner and one homemaker. These are large, important problems—problems I do my part to try to chip away at, but that often leave me feeling small and paralyzed.

But I can, in this moment, kiss the top of my daughter's head. I can say, "I know *exactly* what you mean, because sometimes I love to play alone, too." I can assure her she should never feel bad about telling someone she wants to play alone, because playing alone is a wonderful, important thing to do. I can rise to my feet and walk out of the room, delivering her back to the sea inside of her.

As I do, it dawns on me that perhaps my most pressing work as a mother isn't only to gather my children close, but to provide them space to disappear. It dawns on me that while attachment is one form of maternal care, so, too, is release from attachment. It dawns on me that the most loving thing I can do for my children might just be to appoint myself protector of their inner lives, custodian of their autonomy, fierce and stout defender of their solitude.

It's hard to give to your children what you have not been able to give to yourself. This, too, dawns on me.

One evening, I slide into bed next to Paul, who is already under the covers reading. I want to tell him something, something I've tried to tell him before, but that has come out sketchily, obliquely. "It's all so endless," I might have said, or "I'm so exhausted." Or I might not have said anything at all, but instead huffed my way around the house, making myself intolerable. I've come to understand that a marriage, no matter how strong its foundation, can never fully seal itself off from the culture in which it exists, whose forces seep like floodwater into its crevices, rising up in the silences that can't quite be breached, the thousand simmering resentments that can't quite be named.

I shift onto my side and look at my husband. "I need more time to myself, away from everything," I say.

It takes some back-and-forth for him to understand that I don't mean a pedicure, or a "Moms' Night Out," or some other culturally sanctioned maternal break. But not too much back-and-forth. And I'm reminded, in a comforting way, that this is the person with whom I've shared my days and dreams and flesh for nearly two decades. I have underestimated how much truth he has heard in my silences, and how much understanding has been waiting for me in his.

I share my idea. "I've been thinking about going away by myself somewhere for the long weekend," I say. "It might give me a chance to clear my head, give me a chance to write."

I feel the press of our headboard against my shoulder, the weight of our comforter over my knees.

"I think," he says, after a moment, "that makes a lot of sense."

I look at my husband, his flecked green eyes, his soft black lashes. With him at my side, I have cracked open a velvet box, sparkling with a million diamonds. I have untied a blindfold, welcoming myself to my dreamhouse. My husband has uttered what are possibly, in their way, the most erotic words he has ever spoken to me. I turn off the light and reach for him.

...

I do not head, like Thoreau, to a lake but to the mountains—a small range in northeastern Vermont where I've found a weekend rental on Vrbo. As I begin the three-hour drive, my mind keeps tumbling down its habitual channels. On Storrow Drive, I remember I must email Paul the Sunday Hebrew school schedule. On the Tobin bridge, I'm gripped by panic that Leigh's homework won't get done. On I-93 North, I wonder what my children are making of my absence, and just *what* is it I'm heading off to do again?

In three hours, a landscape can change entirely, the ground growing steeper and rockier, the road winding more tightly as it narrows. In three hours, I am tracing the path of ancient glaciers curving through shale cliffs and massive pines. Cresting a hill, I see snow-swept fields in the distance, and beyond these, a snow-frosted mountain, and then another. To my left is a creek; to my right, an iron-gray lake, partially frozen. A gust of wind jostles the car and something inside me.

The house is exactly what I'd hoped: quiet and clean, a snug oasis of wood and rug and stone. I unpack my groceries and float from room to room, tasting the firewood air, running my fingertips along the silent wood of the windowsill. Beyond the pane are birch trees and a sky so huge it makes me feel at once small and tremendous. I'm a tiny thing under this sky, but also it is in me, spreading me into panorama.

On the couch, I read a little, write a little. I listen to the tick of the wall clock and the hum of the refrigerator and the low ambient thrum of an undisturbed room. I take a walk. I return to the couch, where I lie on my side and feel blood pulsing in my chest as my mind nestles into itself. Slowly, the sky settles and shadows spread across the room. I begin to notice something inside my belly— a small, gentle wanting—and it takes me a moment to recognize it as the beginnings of hunger. For dinner, I have a bowl of canned soup and potato chips, and no feast has ever tasted more delicious.

That night, I call Paul. I tell him about the stone fireplace, and the birch trees outside my window, and how I walked through crusted snow to the top of a hill. "Thank you for this gift," I say.

"It's not a gift. It's yours," he tells me—and he is right.

I know that this mountain getaway is extraordinary—an escape to solitude far too extravagant to become a norm. But maybe, I think, it could serve as a sort of initiation or intensive immersion. If for three days I can calm the voices of guilt and self-judgment, if I can remember what it's like to be the person I am, maybe, just maybe, I'll have the strength to visit her again, and then again, and then again.

Witch Lineage

When I was twenty-four, I briefly saw a therapist. Externally, my young adult life was going well. In my job as an assistant editor at a New York publishing house, I worked on the sorts of edgy literary books I dreamed of writing. I had a boyfriend and a rented apartment on the Upper West Side that I shared with my best friend. And yet, the sky and trees and sidewalks seemed to me to be covered in a dull film. My knees felt heavy when I walked. Outwardly, my days swirled with book events and interesting people. Inwardly, there was only the thick gray churning of my mind.

I told the therapist about the churning and about how, lately, the smallest setback could tumble me into a pit of sadness and rage. For instance, I couldn't get over the fact that my roommate, Elizabeth, kept drinking my orange juice. When I'd opened the refrigerator the day before and saw that there remained in the Tropicana bottle just a half inch of juice, my body had felt like a large, tender bruise someone had jabbed with their thumb.

Behind my therapist's glasses, her eyes looked flat. She seemed unimpressed by the orange juice, and I didn't blame her. I could hear how small my words sounded. But I didn't know how else to convey the story of my sadness.

"Tell me about your family," she offered.

I described for her my father, my mother, and my older brother. My parents had recently divorced, but I assured her this wasn't my issue, for they'd been happy in the years that mattered. I told her how my brother liked to play the protector, how my father was my go-to person for practical advice, and how my mother seemed more content now, living alone, than she ever had before.

Behind the glasses, a flicker. "Tell me more," my therapist said, "about your relationship with your mother."

I wanted to do well at therapy, to feel I had a psyche worth probing. I sifted quickly through memory. From the millions of moments and sensations and tableaux that made up my mother and me, I pulled to the surface one: a summer day, when I was eight, and she sent me to my room for an entire day. I couldn't recollect my crime, but I was certain, I told my therapist, that my punishment outweighed it. I recalled the thud of my door as my mother pulled it closed, the wet of my pillow, drenched in snot and tears. I recalled staring at my bedspread with its pattern of pink gardenias and hating them for their cheer.

I became, on that office couch, that eight-year-old girl again, the minutes congealing into hours as I wept, raged, stared out the window, drew on my leg with marker. I remembered hearing my mother's voice, distant and muffled, as she called to the dog and answered the phone. I knew the truth about this voice: that it came from a malevolent witch who wished to torture me, and who held in her gnarled hand the key to my prison. I pictured her hunched over a cutting board in our kitchen, her hood sagging over her forehead. She looked, in my imagination, like Dame Gothel from the Rapunzel chapter in my beloved illustrated *Grimms' Fairy Tales*. Dame Gothel with my mother's eyes.

My therapist's eyes narrowed. She was deep in her work now. "That must have felt terrible," she said.

Those slow, oozing hours in my room came back to me, intensified by my adult understanding that ten hours of confinement is, by any measure, an extreme sentence to impose on a child.

Yes, I thought to myself. It did feel terrible.

But *this* moment, I noticed, felt good. I had reached my hand into my murky insides and grasped something hard and tangible, something with contours. I had found something—or rather, someone—more acceptable than an orange juice bottle to hang my pain on.

We learn early that our mothers matter. Our fathers matter, too, of course. But the mattering of mothers is a different sort of mattering, primordial and amniotic. Most of us on earth awakened to life inside the body of our mother, and perhaps we never quite leave her. If we are female, this attachment takes on new meanings as we grow. In the words of Virginia Woolf, "We think back through our mothers if we are women." We look to them for clues to who we are, and what it means to move through the world in female form. We come to understand that our mother *signifies*, and that our relationship with her is a story crucial to pursue.

It's possible I'm particularly sensitized to the psychoanalytic potential of mothers and daughters. I can still picture a hardcover book on my parents' shelf, the title emblazoned across the spine in that trademark declarative font of 1970s book jackets: *My Mother/ My Self.* I didn't need to open Nancy Friday's influential book on mothers and daughters to understand why my mom had purchased it, and what she hoped it would reveal about the source of her life's dissatisfactions. By the time I was a teenager, I'd gleaned that her relationship with her own mother, my Grandma Charlotte, had been complicated. To me, my grandmother was the elegant woman who swooped in from Florida smelling of Cacharel's Anais Anais perfume, who seized my cheeks and called me her *shayna maidel*, whose side I never wanted to leave. To my mother, she was the austere, aproned figure who shooed her from the kitchen when she was small, who dispatched her with bus fare to buy her own clothes, keeping her, always, an arm's length from her love.

Until her parents' deaths in their eighties, my mother referred to her mother as "Mother" and her father as "Daddy." My mother's father, my Grandpa Milton, had eyes that sparkled as he told stories of his childhood romps through the Wisconsin woods. He was tall but walked with a stoop, as if trying, perpetually, to come down to the world's level. He laughed easily and heartily, and when he answered the telephone, he said, "Yyyyello." I can see why my mother adored him.

But there's tremendous distance between the words "Mother" and "Daddy," a panoramic stretch of emotional ocean.

Leigh is nearing her teens now, which means she's saying and doing things unimaginable to me just six months ago, things that alert me to the water rising up between us. On vacation last month, for instance, she pretended not to see me when I handed her the Coppertone spray. "Sunscreen, love!" I said, but my words disappeared into the dunes. She turned her back to me slightly—her pale back, her freckled shoulders, so sensitive and prone to burning. How many times, when she was a baby, had I draped those shoulders with a muslin blanket as she slept against my chest in a carrier?

"Here, let me just do it for you quickly," I said, moving toward her with the spray bottle. She jerked backward, kicking up sand.

"*Stop it*, Mom. I can do it myself."

The sand burned under my feet. My armpits were damp from carrying two beach bags, and Nora had started pulling at my shorts. The bottle hovered between us. "Take. The. Sunscreen. Now," I said. Leigh made a sound in the back of her throat, something between disgust and exasperation. She snatched the bottle and tromped down to the water, spraying a little on herself and a lot in the air.

Later, as Paul and Jacob searched for hermit crabs, I waded into the surf to join my daughters bobbing on the waves, Nora in her floaties, Leigh in her inner tube. I dove under and swam toward them, rising up to see a sailboat on the horizon, a million diamonds glinting on the water. The whole day was ahead of us, and the salty rush of the ocean had opened me to happiness. Yards away, my daughters splashed and giggled, hair slick, chins to the air like otters. "I'm coming!" I called after them.

Leigh turned to me, and then back to her sister. "It's the Mommy Monster," she said. "Swim for your life!" Off they shrieked, feet kicking up foam, hair plastered to their heads, two sisters united against their enemy. This was just the sort of chasing game they love, the sort of game I've played a thousand times with them and their brother: I am a shark, a tiger, a werewolf, a witch.

I'm a thing with suction-cup tentacles, splashing after her daughters with a hungry sucky-face. I am a mommy, and I am also a monster.

. . .

Here are some things I didn't tell my therapist about my mother. I didn't tell her about the time my parakeet died, and she whisked me to the Animal Rescue Fund to adopt a puppy. I didn't describe how she took me for chocolate mice at Delice Patisserie on Wednesdays, or for ice cream sodas at Sundae School on Saturdays. I didn't mention she'd read nearly everything I'd ever written since third grade, scribbling her praise on Post-its and sticking them to the pages. I never recalled how my heart leaped up at the sound of her high heels walking in the front door, or how lying on her bed with my feet under the afghan and my head against her shoulder made the world click into place.

In the movie I began to make of my mother, there was the scene where she demanded I come home from a friend's house to move one dirty plate from the sink to the dishwasher. The scene where I summoned the courage to ask for a training bra, and she pointed out I didn't need one. The scene where she walked in on me, at fourteen, in the dark with a boy, and wouldn't look me in the eyes again for days. As I rose through my twenties, there were other moments to splice into our growing story: the time she snapped at me for planning a father-daughter dance at my wedding, or the time I lay curled on her office carpet, panicked about what to do with my life, and she screamed at me to "get a grip." So many of the other parts ended up on the cutting room floor.

We tend to think our memories are what happened to us, solid and immutable as stepping stones. But often, our memories are what we make of them, truth and need colliding to form the tales we tell ourselves—or the tales we've been told to tell.

• • •

Popular culture takes curious delight in tensions between mothers and daughters. We circle around the celebrity stories: Christina and Joan Crawford, Carrie Fisher and Debbie Reynolds, Frances Bean Cobain and Courtney Love, Drew and Jaid Barrymore, Britney and Lynne Spears. Why do so many of our mother-daughter myths speak of estrangement and rupture? And where are these stories' unnamed fathers hiding out?

Female discord tends to be taken, in our inherited narratives, as a given: sisters fight because sisters fight; women colleagues compete because women colleagues compete; mothers and daughters spar because mothers and daughters spar. But I've begun to question what systems are bulwarked by these rivalries, and whom they serve—for it's certainly not the women and girls embroiled in them. Compulsory heterosexuality, patriarchy, militarism—all of these rely, it seems to me, on the breakdown of matrilineal bonds, and of bonds between women generally.

Now that, as an adult, I've read *My Mother/My Self*, I know that it stresses the importance of separation. To thrive, Friday insists, a woman must forge an identity distinct from her mother's: "The only way to describe symbiosis between mother and daughter after age three is unhealthy." How different this outlook is from that of Adrienne Rich, a contemporary of Friday's, who called the synergy between mother and daughter our world's "great unwritten story." There might be no human relationship, she argued, "more resonant with charges than the flow of energy between two biologically alike bodies, one of which has lain in amniotic bliss inside the other, one of which has labored to give birth to the other."

And yet, of these two perspectives, it's Friday's that seems to dominate our cultural psyche today. Maybe this is because it's useful, in a patriarchy, for women to believe their life's task is to separate from their mothers, the humans who provide our aboriginal experience of female love, intimacy, power, and protection. And so, like a willing Persephone, many of us collude in our own abduction, looking for the maternal failings that might ease our leave-taking. Conveniently, all mothers *do* sometimes fail, because everyone sometimes fails.

There are some failures so profoundly damaging they're beyond forgiveness—physical abuse, gross neglect—but these aren't the sort of failures I'm talking about. I'm talking about the garden-variety missteps a mother is destined to make. I'm talking about the stumbles that qualify as failures only in a culture that treats mothers, in general, as the source of its shortcomings, and gives us license to point to our own mother, in particular, as the source of our own. How many times have I—a mother! a feminist!—witnessed a child behave poorly and reflexively thought, "Where did *that* kid's mom go wrong?" When, at the age of twenty-four, I walked into a therapist's office with the earliest stirrings of the depression that I've come to understand, over two decades, as an unalienable, chemical part of my being, it seemed only natural that she would point me toward my mother for understanding. My gaze had already been eased in her direction.

The literature of self-help offers books to assist in this training. A few weeks ago, I thumbed through some of these at the library, curious what they had to offer. In *Our Mothers, Ourselves: How Understanding Your Mother's Influence Can Set You on a Path to a Better Life* (not to be confused with *My Mother/My Self*) psychologists Henry Cloud and John Townsend propose there are six "mom types," each guilty of a different transgression. There's the "Phantom Mom," who's emotionally unavailable, and the

"China Doll Mom," who's too emotionally identified. There's the "Controlling Mom," who feels threatened by her child's autonomy, and the "Trophy Mom," who lives for her child's accomplishments. The lesson I gleaned from these authors—both men, neither mothers—is that a mother must be everything, but not *too* much of anything. Should she fail to act within this narrow margin, they warn, the "relationship that should provide the bedrock of emotional security...ends up providing just the opposite—the seeds and paths of emotional insecurity."

In the summers of my own childhood, after long family days at the beaches of Long Island, I often came home with skin scorched enough to give me chills, skin that screamed for vinegar baths and eucalyptus gel and chewable aspirin. Where in God's name was my mother with the sunscreen, I've wondered so many times since I've been old enough to give form to my resentments. (Only now does it occur to me to ask where my father was—the answer to which is probably napping with a beach towel over his head, as he loved to do, while my brother and I drizzled his sleeping toes with sand.) Now, I smear layers of SPF 70 on my children's wincing faces. I chase after my oldest with the spray can, smothering her in aerosol.

How much sunscreen is too little? How much is too much? And is it in fact possible, ever, for a mother to get this volume right?

When I went into labor for the first time, my mother drove three hours from Connecticut to be by my side. It had been six years since Paul and I had married and moved to Boston. In this time, my mother's and my relationship had grown lighter, airier—less charged, but also less textured, our conversations pattering over surfaces, never quite sinking to the depths they once had. We spoke of our weekend plans, or the new couch I might purchase, or whether the leaves had changed colors in your area, too? The frictions of our earlier years had ended not in some dramatic break or climax, but in this—a tepid coexistence across hundreds of miles. In times of grief or joy, confusion or epiphany, it was my husband I now ran to in celebration or curled up against under the afghan.

Part of me accepted this shift as the way things are as one moves through life's stages and begins to build a family of her own. But inside me, too, was a longing for my mother I can best describe as homesickness, her absence from the deeper spaces of my life leaving me with a vague and chronic feeling of exile. Now, as my own baby began her slow descent into the world, here was my mother in my doorway at midnight—her hair swept back, as usual, in tortoise combs, her lips bright with her usual frosted mauve lipstick, entering our apartment as she enters all spaces: without fanfare. Paul, who'd been beside me for twenty-three hours of slowly progressing contractions, slipped gratefully off to bed. My mother sat with me through the night as I crouched on all fours on my hardwood floor, moaning through each deepening wave of pain. And when the time came, in the blue-gray fog of early morning, to head to the hospital, she followed us there, our little caravan lighting the empty streets.

When Leigh was born, I held her impossible body in my arms, and then Paul held her in his arms, and then my mother held her in her arms, and for the next few dreamlike weeks, these arms, these people, were the only embrace, the only bodies that mattered. My mother was with us when we drove our baby home; when we placed her for the first time in her bassinet; when we fumbled through her first bath. And when Paul went back to work, she was with me still, gathering up the baby when I needed a shower, returning the baby when she needed to nurse, tidying and humming to the baby while I slept. The February wind rattled the windowpanes, but inside the apartment, the air was padded with down.

The morning of my mother's scheduled departure, she stood with her suitcase by the door, her black puffy-coat hanging open. I held my baby daughter in one arm—and with the other, I hugged my mom goodbye, the three of us locked in a quiet huddle. When we pulled away, I saw that my mother was crying. She did not want to go. Something had happened inside these weeks, inside this apartment, while this still unfamiliar creature floated between us. My mother and I had been two frayed threads, dangling in the air. My daughter had slipped in like a third strand, braiding us gently together.

I closed the front door and listened to my mother's bag bump down the stairs. I was filled with overwhelming tenderness for this woman who had birthed me, raised me, brought me to this moment. The barrier that had grown between us had, if not quite disappeared, then cracked and loosened, like an outgrown carapace. It was as if, in becoming a mother, I'd discovered the fullness of my daughterhood—which was connected, as if by a long umbilical cord, to my newborn motherhood. It was as if my daughter had split me open, and I'd been turned inside out.

How easy it was to imagine, in the first weeks of Leigh's life, that I would never fail her. Every part of her being—the soft hill of her belly, her blinking eyes, her parted lips with their tiny slips of breath—insisted that perfection was possible, and that it could be sustained and nurtured if only I remained up to the task. Not every woman, perhaps, was up to this task, but my God, I would be. New to motherhood, I had the conviction of a convert, the enthusiasm of the freshly arrived.

The hardest thing for me about motherhood—eleven years and two more children later—has been the gap between this desire and reality. The truth is I have failed my children again and again. I've failed them with my laziness, my preoccupation, and my insensitivity. I've failed them with my habit of murmuring "Oh!" and "That's funny!" while they tell me stories I cannot bring myself to focus on. I've failed them by rushing them past ant hills, past robins' nests, past the imprint of copper leaves on the rain-washed sidewalk, for no purpose other than *getting going*. I've failed them by comparing them to others, because look how polite Miles is and how Julia hustles like wildfire to get open for the pass and why can't you say *please* like that, hustle like that, too? I've failed them every time I've forced their squirming torsos into car seats, wrangled their flailing bodies up the stairs, gripped their arms more tightly than I should. I've failed them by snapping, shouting, and worst of all—out of all proportion to the cause, rising out of some hideous, stifled place inside—screaming at them at times with a rage so unbridled it terrifies even me.

Can I redeem myself if I describe my love for my children, heavy and silver-dark as mercury, so dense at times that it traps my breath in my chest? Let me tell you about the songs I've sung them, the stories I've told them, the picture books I've read so many times I have them memorized. Let me describe our traditions: the lighting of Shabbat candles on Fridays and the double-layer cookie cake on birthdays and the sharing of our day's highs and lows before we turn out the lights. Let me conjure the months I nourished them with nothing but milk from my breasts—gallons of myself, drained away in a million tiny sips—and the hours I've spent soothing their fevered bodies. Let me speak of the sacrifices I've made: the desires I've tamped down, the career I've delayed, the dreams I've tucked away in service of their desires, their passions, their dreams.

Ah, but look. Already I find myself slipping from tenderness toward something more toothed and suspect, sabotaging my own defense. So you see, it is not so easy to separate the angel from the witch, the goddess from the monster. Our goodness has made monsters of us all.

In her memoir *Mom & Me & Mom*, Maya Angelou recounts how her mother sent her brother Bailey and her, when he was four and she was three, to be raised by their paternal grandmother in Arkansas. As the siblings enter adolescence, it becomes clear her brother isn't safe in the South as a young Black man, and they're returned to their mother Vivian in California. It's been ten years since they've seen her, years Maya has borne with a quiet but fierce resentment.

Bailey swiftly settles back into his mother's orbit—but for Maya, the reunion is more complicated. "He had forgotten everything," Angelou writes, "but I remembered how we felt on the few occasions when she sent us toys. I poked the eyes out of each doll." Her hurt and anger have made her deeply wary of the woman who abandoned her, whom she insists on calling "Lady" rather than "Mother."

Even as Vivian works to build Maya's trust, there are moments when she falters magnificently. There's the time she's jailed for hitting a church friend during a disagreement, and the time she lashes out violently at Maya, too, hitting her when she's stayed out too late at night. As Maya matures to adulthood, there are moments when Vivian heroically protects her—from a deranged suitor, from potential harm during her shifts as San Francisco's first Black streetcar conductor. But protecting her daughter from her own volatility is a different story. When Maya tells Vivian that she and her white boyfriend have decided to get married, Vivian not only stops talking to her, but picks up and moves to another city, effectively abandoning her once again.

It would be easy for *Mom & Me & Mom* to follow the usual course of the fraught mother-daughter story, the aggrieved daughter tapping into wells of inner strength to rise like the proverbial phoenix from the ashes of her subpar upbringing. Angelou certainly had enough plot points—abandonment, physical abuse, incarceration, a *second* abandonment—to tell such a story. But what makes this memoir so powerful are the ways it veers off script. Just when you're ready to condemn Vivian, Angelou slips in a quick, redemptive glimpse at her mother's radiant love for her. We see Vivian reacting with graceful mercy when the teenage Maya tells her that she's pregnant; we see her climbing onto the delivery table to grasp Maya's hands as she births her baby; and we see her stopping Maya as they casually walk down the street to make this remarkable proclamation: "Baby, I've been thinking and now I am sure. You are the greatest woman I've ever met." Stunned, Maya thinks, *Suppose I really am going to become somebody. Imagine.* As readers, we know how fully this imagining becomes reality—and we're meant to connect the dots between *the* Maya Angelou and the inconsistent mother who believed in her.

I'm not sure I would have loved this memoir as I do if I'd read it in my twenties, before children. As a middle-aged mother with my own mistakes behind me, I find Angelou's spacious portrayal of Vivian deeply comforting. Even when describing her mother's worst moments, Angelou somehow manages to convey a quiet pride in her: it's there in the steady tone of her writing, so constant and unrattled. Sprinkled throughout the memoir are photos of Vivian as she grew from a young mother to a bespeckled grandmother, which make reading it feel a bit like reading a funeral tribute album—an unusual one that highlights its subject's worst traits as well as her best.

At the end of *Mom & Me & Mom*, Maya sits by her aged mother's side as she lies in a coma and utters one of my favorite lines in all of literature—not because of its cleverness or beautiful imagery, but because of the huge, compassionate bluntness of its honesty. "You were a terrible mother of small children," Maya tells her dying mother as she holds her hand, "but there has never been anyone greater than you as a mother of a young adult." What exhilarating relief I feel on Vivian's behalf when I read these words. This isn't a hazy, glossed-over sort of forgiveness, but a forgiveness made all the more poignant for being qualified. It isn't Angelou's praise of her mother that makes my eyes water. It's her praise and criticism *in combination*, her wide-armed acceptance of paradox.

Sometimes, lately, when I hold my memories of my mother and me up to the light, it's as if they've rotated ever so slightly, showing themselves from a different angle. Is that a glimmer of devotion

I see in my mother's calling me home to rinse a plate? A flash of helplessness in her demand that I "get a grip"? When my mother sent me to my room from morning to dusk—something she had never before done, and never again would do—why had *that* day unfolded, for her, and so for me, in the particular way it did? This question is what interests me now.

It didn't occur to me until recently that to answer this, all I needed to do was pick up the phone and ask my mother. And so I did. Not only did she remember this punishment, but she remembered the triggering event. "You kept sneaking into your brother's room and going through his things," she told me. "This had happened maybe three to five times, and I kept telling you not to, but you just kept doing it. I remember feeling completely frustrated—the situation felt totally uncontrollable to me."

"And so that's when you decided on a day in my room as a punishment?" I asked.

"Oh, no," she said. "No! The punishment came from my rage. It was not at all a contemplative action."

"Did you remember feeling bad at all?" I asked. "Did you regret doing this to me?"

She was quiet for a moment, as if trying to sink into memory. "I remember coming to visit you in your room a couple of times," she said. "I can't imagine I didn't bring you meals!" She paused, choosing her words. "When you were born, Nicole, I was so thrilled. I wanted a daughter so badly. I remember bringing you home from the hospital and making a pact with myself: *I'm going to make sure my daughter and I are close, no matter what.* As you grew, I loved so much about mothering you," she said.

"But," she went on, "if I had to do it over again, there are so many things I'd do differently. I feel such regret that I wasn't more available for you, that I didn't spend more time with you, that I wasn't more, I don't know, *involved.* I never intentionally wanted to do anything to harm you. But sometimes...well. Sometimes it just didn't work out that way."

I listened to my mother, to this story she'd been telling herself for who knows how many years about her mothering, a story laced with sadness and remorse. I felt this story's sting, but not as her daughter, for the remote mother she described wasn't the mom I recalled. I felt it as a fellow mother, trained, like her, to see myself as lacking. For when we absorb that our mothers are to blame for our struggles, we also absorb the inverse: that we are to blame for the struggles of our children. Which is why the condition of motherhood is, for so many women, the condition of feeling that your every action might somehow harm what you love.

The phrase "mom guilt" is sometimes used to describe this feeling. Like many phenomena associated with "moms" and "mommies," this term brings to mind a small, cute thing—pesky, but ultimately harmless (as in, *I fed my children chicken nuggets three nights in a row—#momguilt!*). It also implies that this guilt is self-inflicted (as in, *We're so hard on ourselves with our #momguilt!*). But behind this anodyne version of maternal self-judgment often lies a painful and corrosive shame. Anyone who knows shame knows its destructive powers, how easily it edges into rage. And because there's no acceptable space for mothers to direct this rage, it frequently gets directed at the very children we long desperately to do well by—because they are there, because they are small, because they cannot help, in their humanness, to provoke feelings in us of deficiency. Because we mistake them for the cause of our shame, when really, they're the victims of its fallout.

As I talked on the phone with my seventy-five-year-old mother, I pictured her curved shoulders against her pillows, her hair in combs, her dog at her feet, and I felt intensely the futility of her self-admonishment. "But, Mom," I said. "Think about it. Whatever you think you did or didn't do, I'm *okay*. I mean, I have my issues. But also, I'm *fine*. I've turned out pretty okay."

"Yes..." said my mother. "Yes...I suppose that's true." And then she laughed—quickly, brightly, as if caught off guard by her own delight. I told my mother, then, about my own maternal shame, how it's with me always, like a parasite gnawing at the edges of my days. She listened without judgment, even though my children are her grandchildren and therefore, in her eyes, perfect, and I could see how the feelings I described might be unsettling to her. We stayed on the phone for an hour—two mothers, and two daughters—traversing, together, the landscape of our imperfections. When we hung up, my mom said, "I'm so glad we had this talk. I could never have had this conversation with my mother."

Later, as I drove my kids home from school, I turned up Sirius FM and belted out Prince. The three of them rolled their eyes at my '80s music and terrible singing, but I'm certain, too, that part of them loved it. When we passed JP Licks, I surprised us all by pulling over. We ate our ice cream on the bench outside, where I remained unrattled when Jacob and Leigh started bickering. The sun warmed the back of my neck as I wiped a dribble off Nora's chin and swallowed a perfect spoonful of mint chocolate chip, wondering at the small, surprising forms that progress can take.

My friend Mira, who has two elementary school-age girls, recently said to me: "Isn't it strange to think that our daughters will undoubtedly resent something about us when they're grown up, and yet we have no idea now what that thing will be?" Mira is a psychotherapist, and like me, fixated on the unseen things under surfaces.

What kind of witch will I be? Only time will tell, as my actions and my daughters' personalities and experiences converge to shape the stories they weave about me. It's an uncomfortable thought, imagining one of them, years from now, describing for a friend or partner or therapist the ways I drive her mad, the ways I've caused her pain. Which memory will Leigh point to? The time she woke with a migraine in the middle of the night, and I was powerless to help her because I'd put off replenishing our Motrin? The time she rushed through her science homework and I made her do it over, twice, tyrannizing her with my outsized work ethic? Or will it be some future injury I've not yet inflicted but that will stay with her year after year, reminding her what her mother could never be for her?

This last thought is enough to make me fall down on my knees and commit my whole self to never again doing anything as a mother that is less than absolutely loving, absolutely virtuous, and absolutely good. But of course, this is impossible. I suspect the best hope I have of creating a happy future for me and my daughters is to tell them in blunt terms what age has shown me about the happenstance of villainy. I suspect the best hope I have is to say, *I love you, and I'm always trying to do what's best for you. But sometimes it just doesn't work out that way.*

Which are more or less the exact words I spoke to Leigh yesterday morning, as I drove her to school, moments after shouting at her for dawdling on her way out the door. Through the rearview mirror I saw the corners of her mouth curve upward slightly—in a smile? A smirk? It was hard to tell.

Hag of the Deep

The neighbor boys were threatening to kill each other again. They stood face-to-face in their swim trunks, swords raised, bellies arched toward the sun. The brown-haired one lunged first, whacking his redheaded friend across the hip. The redhead stumbled and then recovered, swinging his plastic blade at his friend's neck. *Smack, smack. Stumble. Smack.* Our whole vacation, this battle had been raging outside our little rented beach house.

Paul walked into the kitchen as I watched from the window. "I can't believe there are parents who actually *give* their sons swords to play with," I said.

We were newlyweds, years away from having children of our own, but already I had enlightened ideas about how we would raise them. The two of them—always, I imagined two of them—would be good, kind kids with unapologetic smiles and quirky interests. Our daughter would grow to be brave and self-possessed. Our son would be unafraid of the color pink. As a child of the 1970s, I'd grown up listening to Marlo Thomas's *Free to Be...You and Me* album on my tape deck, learning early that girls could win races, that boys could like dolls. In college, I'd taken enough women's studies courses to qualify for a minor. I knew a few things about gender and patriarchy—things that our neighbors, who sunned themselves in lawn chairs while their sons pretended to slay each other, clearly did not.

Paul glanced out the window as he opened the fridge. "I don't know," he said. "They're just kids. They're just playing."

"Playing at hurting other people's bodies? Playing at aggression?" The stakes of this disagreement felt strangely high to me, as if the boys we were discussing were our own.

Paul shrugged. "I think you're taking this a little too seriously."

I was not, I was certain, taking this too seriously. But it's also true that I tend to take things seriously, and that my seriousness is like a leaden cloak I often yearn to be free of. All my husband had wanted was to check out his lunch options, and here I was nudging him toward an argument over the rearing of our nonexistent son. I took a breath, willing myself to relax. It was a vacation, and I would keep the mood light. Light as sea spray, light as cloud wisps, light as the kite that darted high in the distance, determinedly flapping.

The first time I saw a boy make another boy bleed, I was in high school. My brother and I had snuck off to a Manhattan bar known for its lax carding policy—the same bar where, five years earlier, the infamous "Preppy Killer" caroused with Jennifer Levin before strangling her in Central Park. But we weren't thinking about that as we huddled around a table with friends, downing shots while the Red Hot Chili Peppers banged in our ears. Mike, my brother's oldest friend, held court, telling stories that had us doubled over. Mike was a hulking guy with a deep, warm laugh and perpetual bedhead, and though my brother often said he had a dark side, I'd never seen it. I'd always adored him: the way he called me "Nic," the heft of his arm as he pulled me in for a noogie.

After last call, everyone trickled out onto the humid sidewalk, loitering and mingling. And then suddenly, to my left, commotion. A shout. The crowd contracted into a circle. I stepped closer and peered through a wall of shoulders.

In movies and on TV shows—the only place I'd witnessed fist-fights—opponents moved deliberately, athletically, their choreo-graphed punches delivered with precision. What I saw before me now was terrible in its sloppiness: Mike, heaving and wild-eyed, his big arm crooked, his piston fist driving into some other kid's face. The kid jerked and stumbled backward, and Mike followed, sweaty and bloody-knuckled. More spastic jabs at the ribs, the gut. The vacuum-suck hush of the crowd as the boy went down. And then it was over. Someone pulled Mike away. The boy lay heaped on the pavement.

I didn't want to look as the boy wormed himself to the curb, or as he sat hunched, catching his breath. Scrambled hair, dazed eyes, blood-smacked cheeks. *Fuck*, he moaned, and spat into the street. Red teeth, blood drool. But also: freckled forehead, jug ears, smooth skin, round knees. I noticed his shorts, his sneakers. I thought: *He liked these sneakers, and someone bought them for him.* I thought: *He's worn these shorts before, and someone washed them for him.* It was these thoughts, and not the blood, that made me feel suddenly ill.

I could never look Mike in the eyes again—not when I bumped into him in our kitchen eating Doritos, not when he tried his kid-sister-ribbing routine. He'd betrayed me in a way that couldn't be reversed, had aroused in me an anger whose source I could not yet pinpoint.

. . .

Paul and I did eventually have a son. We hadn't known Jacob would be a boy, just as we hadn't known his sister Leigh would be a girl. I chose not to learn this information—and Paul obliged me—partly because I love mystery, and partly as a protest against our culture's infatuation with the sex of unborn children. Gender-reveal parties had recently become popular, and every time I saw another social media image of balloons exploding with pink confetti, or a cake sliced open to expose blue filling, I'd thought, *Good God, that will not be us.*

I gave birth to our son in the same hospital where I'd given birth to Leigh. Same starched bedsheets, same beeping machines, same hoisting of knees, same enormous arrival. But when Paul cried, "It's a boy!"—when I saw, suspended in my obstetrician's hands, the tiny curled body with its matted boy hair, its scrunched boy cheeks, its pink and swollen and little and perfect boy parts— here was something different, something new. How impossible it seemed that in the recesses of my woman body, between my curved hips, under my fleshy belly—I had grown a creature so fully and distinctly male. Giving birth to my daughter had been a miracle, yes, but a logical miracle, a miracle of replication. This felt more like a lead-to-gold miracle, a *poof!* and the handkerchief becomes a dove miracle. And so my pride in having performed this alchemy was a different sort of pride.

Maybe I felt something of what women have felt for millennia, across oceans and continents, after producing a boy. Tiller of the soil. Heir to the throne. But here in twenty-first-century America, in the liberal stronghold of Boston, out of my purportedly feminist loins—What soil? What throne?

· · ·

Eight days later, in keeping with Jewish tradition, Jacob was circumcised. How many brises, I wonder now, have been arranged as our son's was, by a stunned postpartum mother who hardly knows the steps she's taking, only that she must take them? I waded into the living room in my nicest maternity dress, my belly still large but now deflated, like a forgotten melon. As our guests made small talk, I drank one mimosa, and then another, my baby boy asleep in the crook of my elbow. Best to keep my heart from thumping in his ear. Best to not let on what was about to happen.

The mohel arrived—a woman, atypically, which is why I'd hired her, as if a female touch might soften the pain of this ritual. But there was nothing soft about our mohel, who pulled me aside for my instructions. When summoned, I was to bring Jacob into the dining room. After, I was to take him away.

At the mohel's signal, I carried my boy forth, past my mother and mother-in-law, through a parting sea of suits. I carried him to the towel laid out by the knife, unsheathed and glinting on the table, and into the arms of Paul's uncle Robert, our *sandek*, who had the honor of holding our son down while the mohel sliced off his foreskin. Robert had performed this same hallowed duty when my husband himself was eight days old. We'd liked this poetic echo, so perfect for a tradition that stretched back to Abraham, his sons, their sons.

I did not watch what happened next—only heard it. The soft rip of the diaper loosened, the murmurs of our son awakened. A quick, choked wail. Then more wails, raw-lunged and furious, growing louder, shriller, until they seemed to burst outward from under my ribs. Were there songs? Blessings? I don't remember. What I remember was the way my breasts ached and leaked as I gathered up my son and scurried away with him—my smuggled bundle—yanking down the front of my dress before I'd cleared the door.

No one had forced this ceremony on me. I'd crafted the email invitation, picked out our son's clothes, and styled my hair. But as I nursed Jacob in the bedroom, his shudders subsiding, I did not feel connected to the generations or humbled by the meaning of the moment: I felt the futile desire to rewind time to the moment I first held his perfect body in my arms and resolved to fight for him.

Mine, I thought as the glider rocked beneath us. *Mine, mine, mine.* Inside this room: warm skin, a glistening mouth, a tiny ear, a trickle of milk. Outside it: the flow of four thousand years, sloshing against the door.

Paul and I didn't dress our son in trucks, dinosaurs, diggers, or superheroes, just as we hadn't dressed our daughter in lollipops, rainbows, unicorns, or fairies. We gave both children cars and dolls to play with. I sang our daughter lullabies and also play-tackled her. Paul pretend-wrestled our son and also swathed him in dryer-warm towels after his bath.

But you cannot stop the world from telling your daughter how pretty her tights are or exclaiming over the muscles of your big, strong boy. You can curate the books your children read and the TV shows they watch, but the gender rules still slip undercover into your children's porous and acquisitive brains.

On Jacob's second Hanukkah, our neighbor gave him a toy Batmobile. Pull the lever on top, and missile launchers spring from the headlights. Push the buttons on the side, and missile launchers spring from the taillights. Pull, push, pull, push. Horrified, I watched my son's little fingers do their work. But I did not take the car away, for under my horror was another feeling entirely: the delicious release of having one's toddler occupied. It wasn't as if this *one* toy, this *one* brief time, was going to ruin him, I reasoned as I slunk off to the kitchen to make dinner.

On Jacob's third birthday, a preschool classmate gave him a three-hundred-piece bin of plastic soldiers and military accessories. "Whoa!" he said as he sifted through tiny cannons and fighter jets and barbed-wire fences. In the pile, I found a Revolutionary War soldier in a vest and breeches, brandishing a musket; a Civil War soldier in a kepi hat, pointing a bayonet; a World War I soldier belly down in invisible mud; a helmeted Vietnam War soldier, launching a grenade. An entire history of state-sanctioned violence lay strewn, in miniature, across our kitchen floor.

After Jacob was asleep, I had to figure out what to do with these warring men. Throw them in the trash, adding to the piles of plastic in our landfills? Give them away to Goodwill for less-fortunate boys to play with—replicating, on a smaller scale, the way real-life military service gets passed off to the less advantaged? In the end, I buried the bin behind a stack of board games in our basement, never, I hoped, to be rediscovered.

A few weeks later I came home from errands to find soldiers arrayed in rows across our coffee table, soldiers stationed on the windowsills, soldiers ducking for cover under our chairs. "Army guys!" our son shouted at me, grinning.

I looked at my husband. He looked at me. "I used to love playing with these when I was a kid," he said, his voice wistful, nostalgic, and also a little apologetic. But not too apologetic. Surveying this scene—the co-created battleground, Paul's legs stretched out before him, our son in his pajamas by his side—I felt as if I'd stumbled into a holy space where I did not belong. They were so absorbed in their project, so content and connected. Wasn't that more important, at this moment, than proving a point?

I headed upstairs to fold some clothes, conquest and decimation resuming in my peripheral vision. *They're just toys,* I told myself. *And our son is just a kid. Just playing.*

There's a conversation some mothers of boys have. I first heard it after my son began attending daycare, at a class get-together. "I always said there'd be no guns in our house, but my son can turn *anything* into a gun," our host said.

"I knew it was a losing battle when I found my son shooting at things with my hair dryer," said another mother.

"You think that's bad?" said a third mother, whose son had recently bitten his toast into the shape of a gun.

Over the years, this conversation has come up more times than I can recall. It came up when Jacob was seven and a twenty-one-year-old man shot down ten people in a Boulder, Colorado, supermarket. It came up when Jacob was five and a nineteen-year-old boy murdered seventeen students and school staff members in Parkland, Florida. It came up when Jacob was two, not long after Tamir Rice, a twelve-year-old Black boy playing with a toy gun, was shot and killed by a white police officer wielding a real gun, highlighting in the cruelest way possible that violent play isn't a universal right of boyhood but a privilege that lives within a hierarchy of power. Not all males, in our culture, can wield pretend weapons with impunity.

Boys who play with guns obviously don't all grow up to commit armed murder. But it's also true that nearly all the people who commit mass murder with guns were raised as boys. This knowledge tugs at me. And yet I can't deny that part of me welcomes these toast-and-hair-dryer stories—the anesthetic permissiveness of them. It's an immense and exhausting responsibility we mothers have, as we stand beneath the tidal wave crushing our sons into acceptable masculine form, to swim with them in our arms against the current. How tempting it can be, as the waters wash over us, to release ourselves to the deluge and declare the task impossible.

Sometimes I tell the mothers about Jacob's old beloved Batmobile, or how he insists on being the bad guy when he plays with his sisters. "I know exactly what you mean," I say to them, because I do.

This is how you begin, when you're a mother, to unknow the things you know, which it occurs to me might be a defining experience, generally, of being female.

I can tell you some other things about boys. Whispered early morning things, choked out middle-of-the-night things. I know the rub of a boy's toes against his sheets, the wetness of his tears on my neck, his slack-jawed silence as he looks up at the August stars. I know how a boy can stoop to pick up a feather, and brush it across his wrist, his cheek. And then brush it across his sister's wrist, his sister's cheek.

I've seen how a boy's face can crumple when he realizes that "crate training" a dog means locking him in a cage, or that the thing in the mouth of our neighbor's cat is a bird. I know how he can fashion a fence from twigs to protect an anthill.

Do I know how a boy can shout and slam doors and storm through the house telling the people he loves that he hates them?

I do, because the boy I know best arrived in the world exquisitely attuned to its chafes and injustices, and so he does all these things. But I also know that the tender nucleus from which my son's explosions burst is the same place that makes us hold up traffic at school drop-off, because one goodbye hug isn't enough, and so back he comes, tumbling into my arms between the two front seats. I know that what we call hate is sometimes love pushed under a rock, love without light and water. "Tell me to what you pay attention," writes the philosopher José Ortega y Gasset in his book *Man and Crisis*, "and I will tell you who you are." How much love is putrefying inside boys this very moment, starved for nourishment?

I know how my son's face lights up when he sees his best friend, Miguel, outside school in the morning. They link arms, backpacks bobbing, noses nearly touching as they speak. This is the unabashed love of a boy for a boy, a love made all the more luminous by the specter of its impending ruin. Only girls link arms, the world will teach them. Real men embrace only with hearty slap, slap on the back to confirm their maleness. On what day, at what hour, will the codes of manhood sever these two from each other—and so from themselves—like an electric fence?

When I complain to Paul about laser-tag birthday parties and the monster truck destruction video game Jacob played at his friend's house, I feel a little like someone trying to alert the neighbors of a hurricane by pointing frantically to a couple of stray clouds. But in their concreteness, these playthings can feel like the best evidence I have of the forces conspiring against our son, a handy synecdoche for a whole too huge to convey.

Paul often reminds me that he was raised on a steady diet of G.I. Joe and He-Man and *Mike Tyson's Punch-Out!!* and he wasn't damaged forever. "Look at me!" he says. "I don't go around hitting people. I don't run through the streets waving a gun." In his own way—a confident and cavalier way I suspect has been honed by his own decades of male conditioning—he means to be reassuring. But he doesn't get it, or doesn't want to. I understand that our son is unlikely to end up with an arsenal, or to stumble out of bars looking for someone to pummel. The fallout I worry about is far quieter, too slow and subtle to make headlines. I worry our son will take up the work the world started on him, slicing away his softest parts in order to belong. And I worry that, in his belonging, he will find himself, in ways that matter most, alone.

"Look at me," my husband says. And I do. I look at his easy smile, his way of making strangers comfortable, his knack for thinking up names for our kids' stuffed animals. I watch the way he slips hair elastics into his pockets in case our daughters need one, drapes my towel over the shower door so I can reach it, and rubs lotion into our son's knees when they crack with eczema.

But I notice other things as well: the way he folds his arms and straddles his legs when talking with other men, the way he strains for height when posing for photos; the way he guns in and out of the highway passing lane. I listen when he jokes—because to say so earnestly would be to admit that he cares—that he has no friends. Me? I have Mira, whose sentences I finish, and Sara, with whom I somehow feel more myself than when I'm by myself. Paul has the work acquaintance with an extra Red Sox ticket, or the dad with whom he occasionally grabs a beer.

There are things Paul doesn't say even to me, silences that pool around him like a moat. After seventeen years of marriage, I still don't feel that I know, not *really*, what it was like for him to lose his father when he was seven, or to watch his mother struggle in the years that followed. I have stood for years in the shallows of these waters, rarely permitted to venture in much further.

In his self-reliance and stoicism, my husband is very much what society expects a man to be. At times, I wish this were not so. If only he could be a little more like Michelle's husband Joel, who writes confessional notes to her in their shared diary. Or like Mira's husband Sam, who teared up at our children's kindergarten graduation. But Paul is not Joel or Sam—and the truth is, if he were, I would not have chosen him.

It was Paul I noticed that Manhattan summer night when I was twenty-five, with his crossed arms and straddled legs and rolled-up sleeves, standing a few feet away at a party. It was Paul I talked with for an hour, the room behind him fading to irrelevance.

At a Hudson Street bar three nights later, he ordered my vodka tonic for me and slipped a dollar into the jukebox to play the song I chose. We discovered that we both took evening runs along the West Side Highway near Battery Park. "We must have passed each other a hundred times!" I marveled.

He cocked his head, dubious. "I'm very fast," he said. "You probably missed me."

He was kidding, in a way, but he was also revealing himself to me, showing me the contours of his prowess. And I thought, *How fucking arrogant! Who is this guy?* But what I did was lean my shoulder closer to his. I wanted to feel just how strong and fast this man was.

At some point, I made a comment Paul found funny. I don't remember what I said, but I can recall perfectly, as if my nerve endings were still reverberating, the smack of his palm on my thigh as he threw his head back in laughter. Because it was in this moment, with the buzz of his handprint on my leg, the sureness of his laugh in my ear, and the drink he'd bought me in my hand, that I understood with utter clarity that this cocky, manly man was the man for me.

In my shadowy one-room apartment, I watched my future husband peel off his shirt, tasted the bourbon sting of his mouth on mine. And there, for the first time, I surrendered myself to his weight, dissolved under his force, savored every patriarchal inch of his body as he pinned my arms to the couch, and I said, "Yes, yes, yes."

This, too, is the woman I am.

My son is eighteen months old, and my mother has come for a visit. The two of us drink coffee as Jacob occupies himself at our feet, darting over here to bang on the table, stumbling over there to grab a toy. "You know," my mother says, her voice rising with pleasure, "there's something very *masculine* about him."

I look at my son. His fat cheeks. His chin wet with teething drool.

"Mom," I say, "He's *one*. He's wearing a diaper!"

She shrugs. "I'm telling you," she says. "He's very macho. He has a swagger."

I roll my eyes. She's being ridiculous, and who even uses the word *macho* anymore? But as I finish my coffee, I watch Jacob, and I think maybe I can see what she's talking about. There's a conviction in his movements that I don't remember his older sister ever having. She has always been more reserved and watchful—and so, my whole life, have I.

As my son trots past, I reach out and scoop him up onto the couch, flipping him sideways and pretending to gobble his neck. "Who's my macho baby?" I say as he screams with laughter. "Who's my little man?"

I don't know where these words have come from, or what to do with them. I realize that they, too, are part of the mother I am.

I resolve to watch for flickers of my son's most tender feelings, so that I might draw them out and teach him to love them. When I'm sick with the flu and he covers my feet with his sweatshirt, I tell him his caring heart has miraculously cured me. When he tries to hide his tears after his stuffed dog goes missing, I tell him how proud I am that he knows how to grieve. Maybe, I think, if I keep cupping his feelings in my hands, stoking them with my words, he'll never learn to be ashamed of them.

One afternoon last year, I surprised my kids with gifts from CVS: three small, lined journals, one for each of them. The girls flipped through theirs and then abandoned them. Jacob, then seven, sat on the couch and examined his, poring over the pages as if they contained untold stories only he could glean, and then asked if he could have a special pen to go with it. *Oh yes, you may,* I thought as I hustled to my desk. *You may have a thousand!*

Over the following weeks he began to refer to this little black notebook as his Love Journal, which he filled with meditations on love in all its forms. I could not make this up if I tried, nor could I reverse-engineer whatever inspiration led him to this project. Here, corrected for spelling, and shared with his permission, is one of his reflections:

Your soul is made of love. You are like a beat. Every time you do something good, you beat faster and grow bigger. If you are hating, let the love take over you. Be peaceful. You must not be used for badness. It could start a battle, the battle could start a war, the war could start something bigger, and so on.

Parenting has often felt to me like a succession of failures punctuated by just enough small triumphs to keep me from succumbing to despair. Reading Jacob's journal stirred in me a potent feeling of victory, because it provided what I most longed for: evidence that my son's heart was still intact. And while it's not my habit to take credit for what blossoms in my children, I took credit for this book, for it was I more than anyone—yes, even more than my husband, for as long as the work of nurturing defaults to women, this will be the case—who had cradled this part of him. The subtext running through every sentence of that journal was my love.

"To my mom," my son wrote on the inside cover. "For always believing in me."

My son is now eight. He wears his baseball cap backward and grinds his Rubik's Cube around in his hands in the back of the car. At school drop-off, he pulls away when I hug him between the seats. Sometimes he ducks when I lean down to kiss him on the head.

The other night he walked into the den as I was writing in my notebook. I patted the couch cushion, scooched aside a little. "Want to write in your Love Journal with me?" I asked, hopeful.

"Nah," he said. "I never write in journals anymore."

. . .

Many cultures have rites for initiation into manhood, some carried out when boys are as young as eight. These rituals often begin with the separation of a boy from his mother by male elders, followed by trials meant to purge him of his juvenile reliance. Becoming a man, they suggest, requires a symbolic death and rebirth—death of the boy born of woman, birth of the man born of men.

I wonder about the untold stories of these boys' mothers. How many, like me, have suppressed a longing to protest the expectations placed on their sons or recoiled at their own complicity in them? The mother who relinquishes her son to a higher purpose is a recurring figure in Western culture, her sacrifice entwined with the idea of "maternal duty." There is the Mary of Michelangelo's *Pietà*, cradling Jesus's body with serene resignation; Hannah, dutifully ceding her son Samuel to the service of God; and every "Gold Star Mother" extolled for her patriotism after losing a child in combat. Historically, a woman's clearest path to heroism, particularly if she is the mother of a son, is to abdicate her primacy and give him over to the world.

And what of the mothers who can't? Things don't usually go well for them, at least not in the Western canon, in which enduring bonds between mothers and sons tend to be suspect. For Jocasta and Oedipus, closeness persists as perversion, and everyone dies. Same for Gertrude and Hamlet. D. H. Lawrence's *Sons and Lovers* evokes the uncomfortably intimate relationship between another Gertrude and her young adult son. When Paul develops romantic interest in a local girl, his mother is wracked with destructive jealousy: "I can't bear it," she cries, burying her face in her son's shoulder, "...she'd leave me no room, not a bit of room."

The enmeshed mother took on new form in twentieth-century matriarchs like Norma Bates from *Psycho* and Sophie Portnoy of

Portnoy's Complaint. Philip Roth's Alex Portnoy, the novel's protagonist, sees his mother, Sophie—whom he describes as both "castrating" and "a packager of guilt"—as the source of his neuroses. His father's meekness doesn't help things, in his opinion: "[I]f my father had only been my mother! and my mother my father!" Alex exclaims at one point. "But what a mix-up of the sexes in our house!" It's a telling statement: Sophie's personality isn't the problem per se, but the fact that it originates in a woman.

When I read *Portnoy's Complaint* in my early twenties, I loved its hilarious family dynamics and exuberant filthiness. If I was troubled at all by Sophie's character, it was in a vaguely second-wave feminist way (What this woman needs is a job!). Meeting Sophie again recently, I still laughed aloud, but now my amusement disturbed me. For all her foibles, I realized, Sophie is basically well intentioned, and her meddling springs from a place of love. She wants what most mothers want, which is to protect her children and help pave the way for their success. By casting her as ridiculous, Roth achieves precisely what his hero longs to, which is to puncture her power. But what makes her mockable are the very qualities for which men are often rewarded: conviction, determination, the dogged pursuit of her ideals. It's possible to see Sophie not as a joke, but as a tenacious mother-hero who refuses to do what the world expects her to do: fade into the background—head bowed, heart muzzled—in humble surrender.

I don't wish to model my mothering after Sophie Portnoy. But I would like to think, as my son shoots upward past two clothing sizes—banging basketballs against his bedroom wall, testing the feel of curse words in his mouth—that the story isn't over for him and me. I'd like to think there's a role for me yet as he journeys toward manhood. Even, perhaps, a heroic one.

In his 1990 treatise in manhood, *Iron John,* the poet Robert Bly makes a handful of solid points, like this one: "It's important to be able to say the word masculine without imagining that we are saying a sexist word." In our particular cultural moment, when it's rare to encounter the word "masculinity" without the word "toxic" preceding it, this rings true and reminds me, against all odds, of a point made by a very different sort of thinker: "We must define maleness," writes bell hooks, "as a state of being rather than as performance. Male being, maleness, masculinity must stand for the essential core goodness of the self, of the human body that has a penis." For me—admirer of the penis, lover of manly men, mother of a boyish boy—this feels like the right call to action. I don't want to teach my son to mistrust his maleness but to cleave to its goodness, driving away what threatens to rot its edges.

It takes great courage, I'm discovering, to help one's children become who they really are. This is the mother journey that calls to me, the heroism I long to summon.

It's late fall in New England, a season of gray, but after days of rain, yesterday was blue and bright. I brought my kids to the playground after school, parking myself on a bench as they ran off.

When I looked up, I saw that Jacob had begun tagging along with a pack of middle school boys. They thumped past me in a ragtag clump, tossing a football, kicking up wood chips. They had floppy hair, these boys, and wore high-top sneakers with lolling tongues. I could see what my son saw in them: They were, if not exactly macho, then splendidly cool. And, though three years older and nearly twice his size, they seemed to actually like him. They called out his name and whipped him their football, bringing him into the fold like a mascot. This didn't surprise me. My son is the sort of person who glides frictionlessly into any room, merges instantly with any group. This ease is part of his nature, but it's also been nourished by privilege: not everyone, in every sort of body, has the freedom to barrel so effortlessly through the world's boundaries.

Who, I thought, as I watched Jacob sprinting with his new friends, wouldn't want to feel, in their one life, so at home on this earth? How I would love to transfuse just a few drops of my son's confidence into his older sister, so that her shoulders might uncurl, her chin lift, her voice ring out bold and unashamed. How *I*— a grown woman, my son's maker—would love to know what it's like to move through the world in his body, feeling, everywhere I go, that I belong.

My son and his crew had begun scaling the fence between the playground and the athletic field. I considered stopping them— there are rules—but didn't, for the day was so sunny, and it was after school hours, and really, what was the big deal? They dropped down on the other side and stampeded away.

When I next looked up, they were clustered at the far end of the field. There was a flurry of motion, a buckling of bodies. A boy was on the ground, another boy kneeling on him, pinning him there. I scanned for my son, scanned for my son. There he was, the smallest, watching. A third boy flung himself down. I saw a hand fly, a knee jerk. Was this a real fight? Play? I couldn't tell, and I didn't care. Something inside me flared like a struck match, lifting me to my feet.

I would not succumb to the pressure of this cheerful day, bullying me into lightness. I would not bear my lot with downcast eyes. I would be—I could feel it in my talons as I sprang from the bench, as I strode on furious legs across the squelching field— another sort of heroine altogether: Grendel's mother, hag of the deep, heartsick with fury and ravenous for justice. I hollered my son's name as I flew over the ground. The boys froze—they could see my wild eyes, my gnashing teeth. They blinked at me in the startled air.

"Come," I said to my son. He had dirt on his pant-knees, pink in his cheeks. He did not come. "Come," I said again, reaching for his hand, but he shoved it into his jacket pocket, glowering at me as he tromped away. I hurried after him, not knowing exactly for what purpose. I followed him over the schoolyard grass, under a Thursday sky, an embarrassing ogre-mother in clunking boots, the only sort of hero I may ever get to be.

Shake Zone

I am seventeen and driving fast on a two-lane highway with the windows open. It's late afternoon, that hour when the day's edges are singed gold. I'm alone, and because I've just recently gotten my license, this aloneness is a thing of wonder. The light in the eastern Long Island sky seems to be telling me something, promising me something. I press my foot to the pedal of my mother's ancient Volvo station wagon, barreling headlong into this promise, into the golden wildness of it.

In a few weeks, I will leave home for college. Maybe it's the closeness of this freedom I feel as I turn up the knob on the radio and sing along to Pearl Jam's "Elderly Woman Behind the Counter in a Small Town," banging my hand against the dashboard, knowing with certainty as I zoom past the Rite-Aid and Joe's Pizzeria that Eddie Vedder is singing to me—to *me*. His thrashing, plaid-shirted body, the same one I've watched him hurl into a mosh pit dozens of times in the "Even Flow" video, is here in this car with me, but instead of falling into the arms of a concert crowd, it is falling into me. I can feel Eddie Vedder against my chest, Eddie Vedder on my skin, and I press my foot down harder on the gas, my heart the most powerful pumping thing in the world. I have shed all that I was just minutes ago: dutiful girl, rule-loving girl,

girl with the anxious knee bouncing with something inside that needs to get out.

I am heading to a party where anything could happen. I could drink a Smirnoff and orange juice, or I could not. I could let my hand brush against Nick Meyer's hand as if by accident, or I could not. I could dance, or not dance, barefoot on the grass with my head tilted back and my arms stretched up to the moon. What I know is that I have endless days, months, years ahead to rub myself up against the moment, to grab the moment by the back of the neck and pull its forehead to mine, to press our mouths hard together.

The AC is broken and the backs of my thighs stick to the car seat, which is hot and seamed with sand. I turn up the volume. I am nearly screaming now. I can feel the bass in my ribs and something spreading deep in my belly that's like joy, but dangerous. Power? Desire? Maybe both. This is what it is to be seventeen years old, the whole night—and my whole life—ahead of me.

There is no precise moment when my whole life stops being ahead of me. This girl in the car believes she will never *not* be this young. And for a long time, she is nearly right.

In college, she is young, with her full, round face and her late-night conversations she's certain no one has had before, and her pack of Marlboros a day because only old people die. She dances on tables, takes road trips to Montreal on a whim, flirts with her English professor, has sex on the Arts quad in the middle of the night. In her mid-twenties, she is older, but barely. At night, she wears stilettos with dagger-sharp toes and jeggings that cling to her hips. And in the day, when she stands in front of a classroom of high school juniors teaching *Othello,* she feels she is playing make-believe, for she knows inside she is pretty much still one of them.

Meeting the man who would become her husband doesn't age her, nor does marrying him. You should have seen her gown! In that period of the early aughts when all the brides wore satin A-lines, her dress is drapey and diaphanous, with a plunging open back that requires she go braless. This works because her breasts are young and pert and can hold their own.

Turning thirty barely registers. And while she knows on some level, when she becomes pregnant and gives birth at thirty-three, that she has reached a new life stage, it's easy to believe she's still more or less young. There's so much newness in having a child, after all, so much abundance. She has another baby, and then another, which means she spends most of her thirties with her belly swelling or a baby at her breast, her body reminding her, over and over, that it's luxuriant and fruitful.

Then one morning, after all of her babies have left her womb, she walks from the train to work through downtown Boston. She feels fresh and brisk, her hair smelling of peach shampoo, the coffee in her hand filling her with certainty that the day is hers to conquer. She crosses Tremont Street and bounds onto the sidewalk, where she comes face-to-face with the glass façade of a building and the reflection of a woman she is startled to discover is her. Could this possibly be her mouth? On either side are two grooves she's never noticed before, the skin around them slack and slightly drooping. She touches her fingers to her face to confirm. These eyes are her eyes, alright—they're looking right at her—but the half-moons below them are darker than she's ever imagined possible. She walks on, eager to put distance between herself and this evidence that somehow, somehow, time has reached her. She knows, of course, that no one escapes time. But she sees, in this moment, that she has until now held a buried faith that maybe she *could* escape it—that her minutes might magically slip past her body unregistered.

She returns that evening to a porch littered with strollers, her three kids, a pile of school forms. In the kitchen cabinet is the bottle of Caltrate 600 her internist has prescribed to prevent osteoporosis. On her desk calendar is an appointment for a mammogram. On her head are so many gray hairs they can no longer pass as highlights. When she undresses for bed, she notices, most of all, the way her breasts lie flat against her ribcage.

There's no graduation from youth, no clear before and after. Her whole life, she was not in the after, and by the time she realizes she *is* in the after, she is already squarely there.

One afternoon, my friend Michelle calls to tell me a story. The night before, she'd been walking to meet friends for dinner. An evening away from her kids is a rare treat for her—as it is for all my mother friends—and she'd dressed for the occasion: lipstick, knee-high boots, and her favorite jacket, a creamy suede number with a faux-fur collar. As she crossed through the park, passing the basketball court, a boy of about fifteen suddenly appeared before her. "Excuse me," he said. "Are you a MILF?"

"I was so caught off-guard!" Michelle tells me. "Clearly, his friends had put him up to this."

It's been so many years since I've heard this term that it takes a second to register. *MILF*, I say to myself. *MILF*. And then, I think, *MILF?!* This acronym is exponentially more jarring to me now, as a mother, than it was in adolescence. My girlfriends and I didn't use this term back then. It belonged to the boys, and they alone had the power to bestow it, or not bestow it, on our mothers. Lindsey Corvolo's mom, with her endless legs and frosted blonde highlights, was a MILF, as was Amy Pollack's, who once famously danced with the DJ while chaperoning our eighth grade mixer. My own mother was occasionally deemed a MILF— "in a Charlie's Angels sort of way," my friend Danny Farber once said.

Did it matter that Danny was fourteen and had never had sex with anyone, let alone a grown woman? No. The point wasn't that such an encounter was possible. The point, for these boys on the cusp of manhood, was to claim the full breadth of their right to define the female body, to show that no woman fell outside the range of this right, even those thirty years their senior. The word "fuck" is key here. "Have sex with" wouldn't do. The crudeness of "fuck," its hard consonants, with their connotations of force, provide the necessary contrast with "mother" and all the virtue and tenderness this word implies, upending the common understanding that a mother—by dint of her age, her experience, her matronly status—is no longer an object to be desired.

"Wow. I haven't heard that term in so long," I say. "It's such a sexist term, if you think about it."

"I know!" says Michelle.

"And sort of disgusting."

"Seriously."

"What did you say back?"

"Nothing, really. I just sort of smirked and walked on." We're both quiet for a moment, and then she says. "I wonder what it was that made him single me out." And then, "I did feel sort of sexy in that jacket."

When we end our call, I scoop globs of Nutella onto three plates and herd my children into the kitchen for their snack. Leigh comes to the table with her comic book and starts to read me a funny bit, but I can only half-listen. What I'm thinking about is this: If it had been *me* walking through that park last night, would I have been called a MILF?

For the next few hours, I am preoccupied by this question, until it becomes impossible to hide from myself that, while I categorically object to the term MILF, I very much want to be a MILF. For it is one thing to know something intellectually, and it's an entirely different thing to know it in the part of you that makes you crane your neck to see yourself from behind in the mirror or spritz yourself with Victoria's Secret Eau So Sexy body spray before leaving your house. I look down at my soft thighs in their faded leggings, the raised veins crossing the backs of my hands. I run my palm over the pleated skin of my stomach. I cannot assess what it is that I am.

That night, I turn to Paul as we're washing up for bed.

"Do you think I'm a MILF?" I ask

"A MILF? Of course you're a MILF."

"Why do you say that?"

"Well, you're a mother," he says, as if this is the simplest, most obvious truth in the world, "and I want to fuck you." He is being funny, but also dead-serious. Standing beside my husband at our sink, I feel desired, loved, and grateful anew that I have chosen *this* man to be my life partner. But I do not feel my question has been answered.

· · ·

A few months before my fortieth birthday, I decide I would like to run the Boston Marathon in under four hours. I have never before felt moved to run a marathon, let alone swiftly, and I can hardly understand what motivates the nubile college women who breeze by me during Saturday training runs up Heartbreak Hill. What could they have to prove? My motivation has everything to do with the fact that I'm done having babies, which means I'm no longer a "new mom," dewy and radiant, but simply a "mom." I do not long, generally, to run a marathon. I long to be a sleek, Lycra-encased, gravity-defying mother of three who is running a marathon.

I may not be a fresh-faced ingenue, or a supple twentysomething, or a glowing bride or new mama, but I've begun to see that all hope of feeling young and relevant isn't lost—as long as I can conquer that last bastion of female desirability available to mothers and become a "hot mom." This won't be easy, given the significant investment of time and capital hot mom-ness requires. But my mind keeps replaying a comment my friend Laura made when we moved our family from Boston to the suburb where she lives with her family: "It's so depressing how all the mothers out here have let themselves go. You'll see," she said. "It's like they've all just given up." I picture a line of pouchy women in salt-stained snow boots, waiting at school pickup for the children into whom they've funneled all their verve. I feel, suddenly, that it is vital I not become a mother who has given up.

Laura wears fingerless gloves and motorcycle jackets and goes three times a week to the local Pure Barre studio on her way home from work. What I know of barre, a high-resistance exercise regimen based loosely on ballet, calls to me in the same way actual ballet called to me as a little girl, as a doorway to feminine litheness and grace. One evening, I accompany Laura to a class, and though I'm technically past the one-year postpartum mark, I'm offered the special "Baby Bounce Back" package, which helps me believe the outlandish sum Pure Barre will still cost me is reasonable. Plus, isn't it only right that I prioritize my wellness, so that I can remain healthy and able for my loved ones far into the future?

I enter the dark, carpeted studio and join the corps of women lined up at the barre. I learn that to "tuck" means to curl your pelvis under; that to "pulse" means to stand on the balls of your feet and bounce your knees; that the "ledge" is the place where the back of the thigh meets the butt, and that by working this area hard enough, I might develop the trademark "Pure Barre Ledge," defined and taut. I learn that the goal of every exercise is to reach the "shake zone," which is when your muscles start trembling and your limbs start wobbling, proof that your body is transforming.

As I attend more classes, I notice that no matter which instructor I have, she is always approximately twenty-four years old, with flawless skin and shiny hair. The health and shine of the Pure Barre instructors' hair is so consistent that I begin to wonder if this is a requirement of the job. I can think about things like this during Pure Barre because, for the most part, it's very repetitive and predictable. Unlike other group exercise experiences—Zumba, with its collegial dance routines, or even yoga, with its open-hearted reaching toward transcendence—Pure Barre is only what it is, a formation of women staring at the mirrored wall as they "Lift, Tone, and Burn" themselves into shape.

I do not like the parts of class when we look in the mirror. I like the parts when we close our eyes and the techno swells and we push through the "final ten" counts, working "deeper and deeper," "burning it out," until my upper lip is sweating and my muscles are quivering and my bones are shaking and I can feel my ledge lifting higher and my hair growing thicker and my skin turning smoother as the years burn and burn and burn and burn away.

For it isn't long-term wellness, of course, but *this* that brings me back to this dark room again and again. Even as I question this use of time, knowing there are far worthier things I could be doing with it. Even as the blue sky outside shouts to me like a reprimand. Even as part of me also burns with shame.

I am forty-three when I begin to wake up sweating—though this word doesn't fully capture what my body is doing. No athletic endeavor or feat of endurance has ever produced from me such relentless sopping wetness as I now produce while I sleep. Sweat runs in rivulets from my chest to my stomach; it trickles down my back and thighs, drenching my comforter. When I peel off my nightshirt, it drops like a used dishtowel from my hands to the floor.

Some of my friends have also started sweating in their sleep. A few of us compare notes during a birthday dinner and determine that we've entered "perimenopause," which is one of those phenomena you don't know about until you're living it yourself. A woman's fertile years, I now know, don't come to a sudden end, but a protracted, sputtering, sweaty one. We sip our drinks and talk about how getting older is terrible, pointing out our lines and creases and grays, as if comparing battle scars. There's comfort in this camaraderie, and the tone at the table becomes confessional. Meg leans in and points her finger toward the plane of skin between her eyebrows. "Can you tell?" she stage-whispers. "Last week, I got *Botox*."

This news shocks me. I have always associated Botox with fading celebrities and the coiffed ladies with fancy handbags who walk around the Bloomingdales in Boca Raton, Florida, where my mother-in-law lives. Injecting oneself with nerve-blocking toxins for the sake of appearance, I've always thought, is for the vapid and desperate. But Meg, who runs publicity for a nonprofit and spends Saturday mornings with her children at the local food pantry and always has excellent book recommendations, has never struck me as vapid or desperate. Her forehead glows in the restaurant candlelight, smooth as pressed satin.

It's around this time that the skincare products in my medicine cabinet begin to multiply. Not with Ponds and Cetaphil, but rarefied emollients with vaguely medical-sounding names, all of them calling to me with their peptides and antioxidants, and their firming, plumping, anti-aging promises. How easy it is to believe that each will do what the last one has failed to, which is rewind time. I am lured, again and again, by that potent prefix "re-," which whispers to me from each reversing, revitalizing, restoring, resetting, renewing, resurfacing, recovering, and rejuvenating jar and tube. My skin tingles as these concoctions sink in, and I imagine that my collagen has been shocked awake, setting my skin aglow.

My wardrobe also begins to glow. Without exactly setting out to do so, I become the owner of a pewter tank top laced with silver threads, a packet of gold lamé hair ties, iridescent sneakers. When my old black winter jacket starts trailing feathers, I purchase a new one that is also black, but glossy, with silver zippers. My new jacket reflects light boastfully, and when I walk out my front door wearing it, I gleam like a brand new sports car, all shining lacquer and chrome.

· · ·

In 1546, German artist Lucas Cranach the Elder painted *The Fountain of Youth*, a four-foot-by-six-foot depiction of the age-old human fantasy of reversing time. I last saw this painting decades ago, during an undergraduate art history exam, and I can hardly imagine what I made of it as I sat in that dark lecture hall, twenty years old and saturated with youth. One night, sitting at the kitchen table after the kids are asleep, I search for it online. I look at it for several minutes, taking in every detail, seeing what this painting might have to show me.

At the left of the composition, a caravan of wrinkled peasant women enter, pushed over barren terrain in carts and stretchers. They undress and step into the fountain, crossing naked through its waters to the other side. Their hunched figures transform along the way, becoming rosy, fleshy, and full. But it's not just the women's appearances that change. As their wrinkles wash away, freedom seems to rise up from within them. They splash and frolic and glide their hands over their bodies with joyous abandon.

After exiting the water, the women change into sumptuous gowns. On they go from here to a banquet table flanked by dashing men. We see them enjoying an evening of merriment, dancing, and—if the duo hiding behind a bush are any indication—carnal delights. Even the landscape has changed: the boulders on the left have given way to lush rolling hills and open sky. This fountain has granted the peasant women far more than youth: it has granted them wealth, nobility, romance, delight, and endless new vistas to dream upon.

Why are there only women in Cranach's fountain? Surely sixteenth-century men, too, must have craved rejuvenation from time to time, or longed to be restored to some earlier version of themselves. There seem to be heightened stakes for these women, as if their access to pleasure, opportunity, adventure, and possibility hinges entirely on youthful beauty.

In this regard, not so much has changed. My husband, too, is also getting older. But his wardrobe hasn't gotten shiny; his medicine cabinet hasn't filled with jars of creams. He registers his body's shifts, most strikingly, in the way it feels and what it can accomplish. "My pace per mile has gotten slower," he says, tapping his watch as he climbs our front steps after a run. "I don't sleep the way I once did," he tells me, recounting last night's multiple wakings. "I wish," he laments, "that I could enjoy a tequila and soda at night like I used to, without it doing me in the next day!"

When it comes to our experience of aging, the difference between Paul and me is the difference between a person at one with his desires, and a person trained to confuse desirability with desire. A woman who has spent her life jumping through the prescribed hoops of female relevance, and who is now on the brink of aging out of this hoop race, faces something far more formidable and terrifying than a crisis of vanity. For this woman, vitality, zest, heat—the very flare and crackle of life as it announces itself inside of her—has depended for years on external stoking. What happens to this vitality when the stoking stops? What stirs in a female body when it no longer stirs others?

Sometimes I think Oprah might help me answer these questions. Oprah and Meryl Streep and Halle Berry and Helen Mirren— the small cadre of female celebrities aging women can look to for inspiration. But even these luminous elders, when they gaze at us encouragingly from magazine covers, often appear in airbrushed form, all signs of history and living wiped from their faces. Is it vitality, or a trick of the camera, that makes them glow so brightly?

Our fear and erasure of the aging woman runs deep, permeating our most basic folklore. She's the crook-fingered hag who kidnaps Hansel and Gretel, the jealous stepmother who plots Snow White's murder, the wizened sea-witch who steals the Little Mermaid's voice. Several times a few weeks ago, Nora appeared at my bedside in the middle of the night, panicked and sobbing: Ursula, she choked out, was under her bed with a knife, waiting to stab her. In the months before that, it had been Maleficent. And before that, Baba Yaga from her brother's *Spooky Stories from Around the World*. The monsters haunting my daughter's dreams have always taken the form of aging women: She has learned, already, to dread her future self.

If they aren't demonized, older women are often stereotyped as bumbling bit characters—or, in the words of the late ageism activist Maggie Kuhn, as "dependent, powerless, wrinkled babies." The protest group Kuhn founded fifty years ago, the Gray Panthers, fought for the dignity of all older people, male and female. But, as a feminist, Kuhn was particularly interested in puncturing assumptions about older women. Since women tend to outlive their male contemporaries by several years, she celebrated the idea of older women forming sexual relationships with younger men, or with one another. "Our sexuality is so influential in determining who we are and how we relate to others," she wrote. "Indeed, it is the material of life and to deny it in old age is to deny life itself."

Last fall, I attended a talent show at my children's elementary school. Sandwiched between a piano performance and a martial arts demonstration was a skit called "The Granny Olympics." A group of fourth grade girls doddered onto the stage in frumpy

229 Shake Zone

sweaters, holding pretend canes, their hair in buns, their skin creased with face paint. They fumbled through a series of sad athletic feats, such as clearing a two-inch hurdle and racing one another while hardly moving. The audience laughed. I laughed. Only later did I think about how in our purportedly equitable and inclusive community, we all wholeheartedly agreed: old ladies are ridiculous!

That aging is shameful and laughable—and the latter years of a woman's life a descent into caricature or obscurity—are truths so commonly accepted they're barely discernible. But they take their toll on women, nevertheless, wearing away at our sense of possibility, narrowing our imaginings of who we are yet to become, mentally shortening our life spans, and leaving us frantic that with every turn of the calendar page, part of us is evaporating.

When I say that I don't want to be a mother who has "given up," maybe what I'm saying is I don't want to stop believing my next hour could hold something more electric than my last. When I say I want to be a "hot mom," maybe what I'm saying is I don't want stop feeling the knock of my heart in my chest, the touch of the breeze on my legs, the caress of the sun on my neck, the flare of want in my groin. When I say that I want to be a "MILF," maybe what I'm saying is time is running out, and I can feel my grip sliding, and *please god*, *please*, I'm just not ready to go.

Perhaps I've given the impression that I spend my days at my mirror, charting the shifts in my skin and contemplating the ticking of the clock. Far from it. For there are bills to be paid and articles to be written and meals to make and children to raise and a marriage to nurture. The thing about aging is that it happens, mostly, in life's background—and yet, its presence murmurs on in the consciousness, like the low buzzing of a broken appliance, constant and quietly draining.

But there are moments—moments I'm training myself to notice—when the buzzing pauses, and a surprising quiet opens up. One morning, reading a review of a new Emily Dickinson biography, I start thinking about my eighth grade English teacher, Mrs. Rinden, who introduced my class to Dickinson and had us write imitations of her poems. I remember the day she hauled in armloads of her own journals to share with us, and how she urged us to start our own, and how I did—right away—determined to fill my pages as densely and triumphantly as she had. Suddenly, I'm startled by a realization: *I* must now be nearly the same age Mrs. Rinden was when she stood before us, silver-haired and smiling with secrets to tell, igniting that place in my brain that hungers for metaphor.

It occurs to me, then, that I must also be nearly the same age as Lydia Fakundiny, my favorite undergraduate English professor, who took us so seriously she scared us into taking ourselves seriously. And nearly the same age, too, as Susheila Mani, my first teaching mentor, when she revealed to me, through her regal example, the power of calm. I'm close to the same age now, it dawns on me, as *most* of the bona fide grown-ups I looked up to in young adulthood: the dignified and self-possessed women— for they were nearly all women—who saved me from self-destructive paths, pointing me toward better ones. When my mind does this temporal somersault, it's not loss I feel but a quiver of hope: Maybe I've lived my way closer to their wisdom and wholeness.

One bright fall morning, I arrive home from a run and see my neighbor Barbara digging in her yard. She wears sneakers and a flannel jacket, her glasses pushed atop her short hair. I am happy to see her. Barbara, who has two grown children, is a former rabbi, the former editor of a Jewish feminist magazine, a psychotherapist, and a writer. Today she tells me about the children's book she's working on—her first. The knees of her jeans are caked with dirt, and I feel I could stand here all day as she squats among her chrysanthemums, patting them into the earth with her soil-streaked hands. I am drawn to Barbara by a feeling I have no precise word for. Admiration, but not just admiration. Respect, but not just respect. In its thrill and intensity, it is, more than anything, like a crush.

"The soul selects her own society," wrote Dickinson, in a poem I may have read in Mrs. Rinden's class. My whole life, I think, as Barbara stands to survey her work, I've been pulled toward women like her, women whose years curve like buttresses around them, women sturdy enough to set the terms of their mattering. Even as I've strained to meet our culture's glossy standards, I have circled around these women without quite even knowing it, as if following some primal instinct, or heeding the call of some archetypal figure of my unconscious: the wise woman, the crone, the great mother. Western culture doesn't typically value or celebrate the female elder. But perhaps, beneath the spangled tank top and flashing parka and layers of skin creams, my soul has been trying to become her all along.

Sometimes, I can already spot her—as if from a distance, through a veil of haze. Her hair is gray, her skin free of makeup. She wears loose clothing and sensible shoes, and when she moves or thinks or acts, she takes her time, letting each moment settle before it passes through her. She eats and drinks with pleasure and relaxes with abandon, her head thrown back on the pillow, her feet on the arm of the couch. She listens fully when others speak, stepping into their words like a seasoned traveler, unburdened by petty distractions. When she speaks, she says only what she means, and her words carry the generous lucidity of truth. She sits down at her desk to write each day lightly, with none of the cramped, hard panic that followed her for years. People come to her for wisdom—and why not? She's been gathering it up her whole life, after all—in the margins of books, in the pages of notebooks, on the surface of her skin, in the knowing folds of her flesh, slackening with age. Some might look at her and say she's giving up. But she knows that what she's doing is letting go.

There is no true "re" in life—no reversing, reliving, or redoing. There is only this moment, carrying the embryo of the last as it unfolds into the next. The wise woman in the haze understands she can never fully return to the girl inside her. She can only take her by the hand and invite her along into the future, teaching her everything she knows.

On an early October morning, I drop my children at school and ease out of the parking lot. I feel a quiet excitement, as I do each weekday morning, in this release into solitude. The hours stretch ahead of me, and I am full of ideas for the article I'm working on. When I get home, I will pour a cup of coffee, open the shades, and get to it.

Steam rises off the reservoir as my car curves by. Sun burns through the clouds, flashing through branches. I open the window, breathing in the leaf-damp air as I stop at the light by the Mobil station. I turn on the radio. There's a quick promo, and then the opening bars of a song. I know it within seconds, the clean acoustic chords accompanied by a searching baritone voice. *I seem to recognize your face.* I reach for the volume.

When the light changes, I press down on the gas, and then press harder. The morning street is empty—only sky and tree-lined road ahead of me. Air gusts into the car, spilling like water over my neck. I am doing thirty-five, forty, forty-five in a thirty, but I don't care because Eddie Vedder is building to something, the air of his breath pouring through the speakers, blowing my hair across my face. I can feel Eddie Vedder on my palms, Eddie Vedder along my spine, and I turn the volume higher as he wails to me about memory and return. The leaves wink orange, the drums bump in my sternum, and before I know it I am singing at the top of my lungs, my jaws flung open to the sky. The words stream out as if they've been stuck in my throat for decades.

Who knows how fast I'm going now. My blood wobbles and my cheeks burn and my voice trembles and my thighs shake as I fly under telephone wires, my shoulders banging against my seatback, my hands beating time on the steering wheel. The people in passing cars must think I'm crazy, a middle-aged woman thrashing back and forth in her minivan, but what do they know.

This is what it is to be forty-four years old, with the whole day—and my whole life—ahead of me.

Memento Mori

A clock, a seashell, a half-empty cup of water. Beside them on Nora's nightstand: the picture book I've finally closed, the lamp I've finally clicked off.

In the dark, her finger traces the back of my hand. "Why are your veins so puffy?" she asks, poking. I tell her that it runs in the family, and that I used to drag my finger over my mother's veins the same way when I was a girl, imagining they were a family of worms.

"One day, you'll have big, squiggly veins like Grandma and me," I say.

I give my youngest child a fat kiss on the forehead. It's meant to signal the end of things, like an exclamation point, or a period, so I can slip away and put this nightly countdown behind me. But she doesn't want a period. She wants a comma. She will do anything to keep me here, listening to my sentences run on. "Tell me another story," she says.

Why not, I think. *Why not?* After all, what waits for me back downstairs? Three unreturned emails and the dregs of a carton of ice cream. I cannot say why it feels so hard to give my child this very small thing she craves. I cannot say why my legs itch to get nowhere, or why the blood in my chest feels like the slow, chugging hand of a clock.

"Let me think," I say, but the only stories I can summon she's already heard. The one about the time I fell on my butt during a high school dance performance. The one about the time I got sick from licking too many honeysuckles. The one about the time I swam in a terrifying pool at the edge of a waterfall. But my daughter has faith in my untapped material. Lately, she's been giving me prompts, like an encouraging writing instructor. *Tell me about a time you got hurt,* she says. *Tell me about a time you made a friend.*

"Tell me about this ring," she tries.

Her fingers land on the gold band I sometimes wear, etched with a pattern of leaves. I tell her that it belonged to my Grandma Beatrice, who died before she was born. I tell her about my grandmother's famous garlic toast slathered with mayonnaise, and how sometimes she hugged me so tight I could hardly breathe. "She left this ring to me," I say.

"Left it to you?" Nora asks, and I realize that though she's eight now and knows many things, she doesn't yet know this expression, or what it means to cling to a loved one's orphaned belongings.

"After she was gone. She made sure it became mine so that, in a way, she could be with me always." I think but don't say, as Nora's night light casts shadows across her dresser, that this ring will likely become hers one day, too.

Nora burrows in deeper, pulling her blanket to her ears. It's getting late, and one of my legs has snuck its way off the bed. I give her a final squeeze, tight as a great-grandmother.

"Have you ever thought," says Nora, "that after you die there's no life in you anymore? You can't think, you can't talk, nothing! You're just gone?"

I am so still, so still. Only my heart moves, a little swelling balloon. Then my eyes, searching for something solid. On the dresser, a pot of wilted parsley. In the corner, a broken ukulele. *All the time*, I think. *All the time. When I walk with the dog down hollow morning streets. When I wake in the middle of the night howling* nooooo *into the darkness.*

"I think," I hear myself saying, "that there's something more we become, the way we can't see what's inside a seed until it grows." I want so badly to believe this that, for a moment, I do. I picture myself as a tree on a sunlit hill. And here is my husband beside me, a sturdy oak. Will Nora be a patch of clover? Leigh a ring of ivy? Jacob a soft clump of moss?

"Well," Nora says, "if there *is* a heaven and you can come down from the clouds, promise to come back and tell me!" She says this as only a young child can, with the good-natured sureness that the time she has left is near Infinity.

"I most certainly will," I assure her.

But for now, I'm still here in Massachusetts, where I'm not a sunlit tree or a golden ring but a middle-aged woman wrapping her wormy hand around her daughter's middle. I press my nose to Nora's neck, my skull against her skull, my mandible against her mandible. The cells of our skin fall to her sheets like dust.

"Tell me another story," she says, and so I do. I tell her about a girl who shrunk herself small and then made herself big again. About a maiden held captive by giants until she outwitted them. About a mother who had so many children she ran away and hid from them. About a woman who got lost in a forest but then found her way home again. The one thing we are certain to become, I think, is a story. I leave myself to my daughter until my throat grows hoarse. I talk and talk until the only person listening is sleeping.

And now I really should go. But I don't. I don't go and don't go until my leg twitches and my eyelids flicker and thoughts pass through my mind in scattered puffs. My last child's blanket is so worn that it floats on my skin. The in-and-out of her breath is the softest breeze.

Here are the clouds, I think. *The clouds are here.*

Tomorrow, I will tell her.

Sources and Works Consulted

KATE CHOPIN, MY MOTHER, AND ME

Chopin, Kate. *The Awakening and Selected Stories*. New York: Penguin Classics, 1986.

Stein, Allen. "The Kaleidoscope of Truth: A New Look at Chopin's 'The Storm.'" *American Literary Realism* 36, no. 1 (2003): 51–64.

The Beatles. "Michelle." *Love Songs*. Capitol Records, 1977, audio cassette.

THE NEW PRETTY

Adiche, Chimamanda Ngozi. *Americanah*. New York: Knopf, 2013.

Cottom, Tressie McMillan. *Thick and Other Essays*. New York: New Press, 2019.

Kafka, Franz. *The Metamorphosis*. Translated by Susan Bernofsky. New York: W.W. Norton & Company, 2014.

Lorde, Audre. "Learning from the 60s," in *Sister Outsider: Essays and Speeches*. New York: Penguin Classics, 2020.

Ovid. *Metamorphoses*. Translated by David Raeburn. New York: Penguin Classics, 2004.

Parker, Kate T. *Strong Is the New Pretty: A Celebration of Girls Being Themselves*. New York: Workman: 2017.

Rich, Adrienne. *Of Woman Born: Motherhood as Experience and Institution*. New York: W.W. Norton & Company, 1986.

Tippett, Krista. "Beauty Is an Edge of Becoming." Produced by American Public Media. *On Being.* March 18, 2016. Podcast, website, https://onbeing.org/programs/2-beauty-edge-becoming-john-odonohue/.

Tippett, Krista. "Music Happens Between the Notes." Produced by American Public Media. *On Being.* September 4, 2014. Podcast, website, https://onbeing.org/programs/yo-yo-ma-music-happens-between-the-notes-jul2018/.

Winfrey, Oprah. "Lady Gaga: Heal Through Kindness." Produced by OWN. *Supersoul Special.* November 6, 2019. Podcast, website, https://www.oprah.com/own-podcasts/super-soul-special-lady-gaga-heal-through-kindness

Wolf, Naomi. *The Beauty Myth: How Images of Beauty Are Used Against Women.* New York: Harper Perennial, 2002.

AS THEY LIKE IT

Bentley, Thomas. *Monument of Matrones.* London, 1592.

Howard, Jean E. "Crossdressing, the Theatre, and Gender Struggle in Early Modern England." *Shakespeare Quarterly*, Volume 39, Issue 4 (Winter 1988): 418-440.

Shakespeare, William. *As You Like It.* London: The Arden Shakespeare, 2006.

Shapiro, Michael. *Gender in Play on the Shakespearean Stage.* Ann Arbor: University of Michigan Press, 1996.

Thirlwell, Angela. *Rosalind: A Biography of Shakespeare's Immortal Heroine.* New York: Pegasus Books, 2017.

Thomas, Keith. "As You Like It." *New York Review of Books*, September 22, 1994.

THE FRIENDSHIP PLOT

Goodsell, Willystine. *A History of the Family as a Social and Educational Institution.* New York: Macmillan, 1915.

Longfellow, Henry Wadsworth. *Kavanagh.* Maryland: Wildside Press, 2014.

Montaigne, Michel de. "On Friendship." Translated by Charles Cotton. HyperEssays.net. January 3, 2024. https://hyperessays.net/essays/book/I/chapter/28/

VERY NICE BLASTOCYSTS

Biss, Eula. *On Immunity: An Inoculation*. Minneapolis: Graywolf Press, 2015.

Brooks, Gwendolyn. "the mother" in *Selected Poems*. New York: HarperCollins, 2006.

Cramer, Maria. "Girl Is Born in Tennessee from Embryo Frozen for 27 Years." *The New York Times*, December 3, 2020. https://www.nytimes.com/2020/12/03/science/tennessee-embryo-donate.html

Dickinson, Emily. *The Complete Poems of Emily Dickinson*. New York: Back Bay Books, 1976.

Pflum, Mary. "Nation's Fertility Clinics Struggle with a Growing Number of Abandoned Embryos." *NBC News*, August 12, 2019. https://www.nbcnews.com/health/features/nation-s-fertility-clinics-struggle-growing-number-abandoned-embryos-n1040806

THINKERS WHO MOTHER

Gilman, Charlotte Perkins. "Why I Wrote the Yellow Wallpaper" in *The Yellow Wallpaper*. London: Renard Press, 2021.

Munro, Alice. "My Mother's Dream" in *The Love of a Good Woman*. New York: Knopf, 1998.

Rich, Adrienne. *Of Woman Born: Motherhood as Experience and Institution*. New York: W.W. Norton & Company, 1986.

Ruddick, Sara. "Maternal Thinking." *Feminist Studies*, Volume 6, No. 2 (Summer 1980): 342–67.

Shafak, Elif. *Black Milk: On the Conflicting Demands of Writing, Creativity, and Motherhood*. New York: Penguin, 2012.

TIKKUN OLAM TED

Martel, Yann. *Life of Pi*. New York: Houghton Mifflin, 2002.

Newman, Vivian. *Tikkun Olam Ted*. Minneapolis: Kar-Ben Publishing, 2013.

Bishop, Elizabeth. "On Being Alone" in *Elizabeth Bishop: Prose, Poems, and Letters*. New York: Library of America, 2008.

Buchholz, Ester Schaler. *The Call of Solitude: Alonetime in a World of Attachment*. New York: Simon & Schuster, 1997.

Chopin, Kate. *The Awakening and Selected Stories*. New York: Penguin Classics, 1986.

Craig, Lyn, and Killian Mullan. "How Mothers and Fathers Share: A Cross-National Time-Use Comparison." *American Psychological Review* 76, no.6 (December 2011): 834–61.

Edwards, Suzanne M., and Larry Snyder. "Yes, Balancing Work and Parenting Is Impossible. Here's the Data." *The Washington Post*, July 10, 2020. https://www.washingtonpost.com/outlook/interruptions-parenting-pandemic-work-home/2020/07/09/599032e6-b4ca-11ea-aca5-ebb63d27e1ff_story.html

Emerson, Ralph Waldo. "Self-Reliance" in *The Essential Writings of Ralph Waldo Emerson*. New York: Modern Library Classics, 2000.

Koch, Philip. J. *Solitude: A Philosophical Encounter*. Chicago: Open Court, 1999.

Lessing, Doris. "To Room Nineteen" in *To Room Nineteen*. Toronto: HarperCollins Canada, 1994.

Sarton, May. *Journal of a Solitude*. New York: W.W. Norton & Company, 1992.

Schulte, Brigid. *Overwhelmed: How to Work, Love, and Play When No One Has the Time*. New York: Picador, 2014.

Strayed, Cheryl. *Wild: From Lost to Found on the Pacific Coast Trail*. New York: Knopf, 2012.

Thoreau, Henry David. *Walden and Other Writings*. New York: Bantam Classics, 1983.

Whitman, Walt. *Leaves of Grass: Selected Poems and Prose*. New York: Doubleday, 1997.

WITCH LINEAGE

Angelou, Maya. *Mom & Me & Mom.* New York: Random House, 2013.

Cloud, Henry, and John Townsend. *Our Mothers, Ourselves: How Understanding Your Mother's Influence Can Set You on a Path to a Better Life.* New York: Zondervan, 2015.

Friday, Nancy. *My Mother/My Self.* New York: Delta, 1997.

Rich, Adrienne. *Of Woman Born: Motherhood as Experience and Institution.* New York: W.W. Norton & Company, 1986.

Woolf, Virginia. *A Room of One's Own.* New York: Mariner, 2005.

HAG OF THE DEEP

Bly, Robert. *Iron John: A Book About Men.* New York: De Capo Press, 2015.

Gasset, José Ortega y. *Man and Crisis.* New York: W.W. Norton & Company, 1989.

hooks, bell. *The Will to Change: Men, Masculinity, and Love.* New York: Washington Square Press, 2004.

Lawrence, D. H. *Sons and Lovers.* New York: Penguin Classics, 2006.

Morrison, Toni. "Gloria Naylor and Toni Morrison: A Conversation." *The Southern Review*, Volume 21, Issue 3 (July 1,1985): 567.

Roth, Philip. *Portnoy's Complaint.* New York: Vintage, 1994.

SHAKE ZONE

Age Stereotyping and Television: Hearing Before the Select Committee on Aging before the House of Representatives, 95th Congress, 14 (1977) (statement of Maggie Kuhn, Gray Panthers national convenor).

Cranach, Lucas the Elder. "The Fountain of Youth." 1546. Oil on panel. Gemäldegalerie, Berlin.

Kuhn, Maggie. *No Stone Unturned: The Life and Time of Maggie Kuhn.* New York: Ballantine Books, 1991.

Pearl Jam. "Elderly Woman Behind the Counter in a Small Town." Track 10 on *Vs.*, Epic Records, 1993, compact disc.

Acknowledgments

Thank you to my agent Anna Stein for her glowing wisdom and steadfast belief in these pages, and to Lynn Grady, Holly La Due, Allison Adler, and Allison Serrell at Chronicle Books for bringing the vision to life.

This book would not exist without the extraordinary English teachers who helped light my path early on. Jane Rinden and Kolia O'Connor sparked my love of language and the promise of a blank page. If it weren't for the singular Lydia Fakundiny and her Art of the Essay seminar, I might never have discovered the essay form, or found the courage to follow its call. I'm so grateful for these teachers—and for all the teachers doing the behind-the-scenes magic of transforming lives.

Heartfelt thanks to the members of the Emerson College MFA community who helped this book take root: Richard Hoffman, Daniela Kukrechtova, Susanne Althoff, Jabari Asim, Richard Haney-Jardine, Katie Bannon, Madeline Sneed, Evan Fleischer, Kristin Crocker, Colin Kirkland, Julia Weeks, and so many others. For the long walks, reading recommendations, and generous attention to every page, thank you to Megan Marshall. I would be nowhere without Jerald Walker, whose perfect essays give me something to aspire to, and whose encouragement has been the wind in my sails. Jerald, I'm so grateful.

I'm indebted to the talented editors who first published some of these words, including Paul Reyes at *Virginia Quarterly Review*, Nancy Holochwost at *The Sun*, Lauren Hohle at the *Gettysburg Review*, Lisa Ampleman at the *Cincinnati Review*, and Donna Talarico at *Hippocampus*. Thank you to the entire wondrous staff of *River Teeth*, whose above-and-beyond support of my work has been a profound gift.

To the authors who gave of their time to offer words of support, thank you for your hugely generous spirit.

For early feedback and writing community, thank you to Michelle Wildgen, Alexis Gargagliano, Erin Servais, E. B. Bartels, Jaime Zuckerman, Tatiana Johnson-Boria, Amy Monticello, Jean Stehle, Jessica Fein, Jen Blecher, Alison Cupp Relyea, Joanna Rakoff, Kelly McMasters, and Susan Schnur. Thank you to the incredible caregivers who made solitude possible: Alice Dillon, Maxine Bergstein, Priya Sagar, and Katia Santos. Thank you to Jennifer Meyer for helping me listen to the small, urgent voice inside of me—and to Geoff Kloske for always being willing to tell me what to do.

"It's not often," wrote E. B. White, "that someone comes along who is a true friend and a good writer." Karen Winn, you are both of these things and more: I can't imagine being on this journey without you. For enduring friendship, thank you to Bronwen Carroll, Carrie Davis, Rachel Englund, Georgia Feldman, Rachel Goldman, Catherine Kim, Matthew Lippman, Liz Molina, Bianca Peskin, Annette Savitch, Phoebe Segal, Ellen Walpert, and Sarah Zimman. Thank you, Jacqui Lipson, for being the sister I always wanted. Sara Walsh, our friendship is one of the great works of my life.

To my mother and father: Thank you for your unconditional love and for believing in me so fully that I had no choice but to believe in myself.

Finally, to my children: You fill my life with purpose, my heart with joy, and my days with hope. Paul, our love is my sustenance. How lucky I am, in this one life, to get to live it with you.

About the Author

Nicole Graev Lipson is an essayist, journalist, and critic whose writing has appeared in *The Sun*, *Virginia Quarterly Review*, the *Gettysburg Review*, *River Teeth*, *The Millions*, the *Washington Post*, the *Boston Globe*, and *Marie Claire,* among other venues. Her work has been awarded a Pushcart Prize, nominated for a National Magazine Award, and selected for *The Best American Essays* 2024. She lives outside of Boston with her family.